Praise for *No Bullsh*t Change*:

'A punchy, practical and inspiring guide for all leaders who wish to transform and grow their team or organisation'
Justine Roberts, founder and CEO of Mumsnet

'*No Bullsh*t Change* challenges the status quo and uproots entrenched ideas of what leadership looks like. Chris Hirst offers a bold and inspiring vision of what the future of business can and should be. We are entering a new era of business where consumers are demanding more, and where the leaders who understand this will be the ones whose companies not only survive but also thrive. *No Bullsh*t Change* offers clear tools on how to do this'
June Sarpong

'A practical and authoritative guide – perfect for our complicated times'
Nicholas Hytner, artistic director and founder of the Bridge Theatre

'I've seen countless business leaders with fantastic pedigrees make career-defining mistakes when managing change in a business. Chris's book provides the sort of leadership lessons and actionable advice that will prove invaluable to the next generation of business leaders'
Andy Silvester, editor of *City A.M.*

'I highly recommend this book to anyone looking for an inspiring and thought-provoking read. The author's personal experiences and insights bring a unique perspective to the topic at hand and make for a truly engaging read. This is a book from somebody who has truly been there and done it, and it shows in the depth and authenticity'

Jack Parsons, CEO of Youth Group

'Not only does Chris Hirst have the experience of leading a remarkable turnaround, he has the wisdom to understand why it worked. This book issues a rallying cry for leaders burdened by permacrisis to take control of their future. As Hirst writes, "if in doubt, do"'

Kate Magee, editor of *Management Today*

'There are many books about leading change. You may recoil at the thought of yet another one. Don't. This book is an easy read, offering simple, pragmatic and achievable prompts. Whether you be novice or expert in the subject, you will find insight throughout its pages'

General Sir Chris Deverell

'Highlighter pens to the ready – practical, plain-speaking and unputdownable guide to inspire you to make change a reality'   Katie Vanneck-Smith, CEO of Hearst UK

'An excellent guide to real-world leadership. Perfect for our turbulent time'

Anthony Scaramucci, founder of Skybridge Capital and former White House Director of Communications

'Clear, punchy, practical and very enjoyable'
Philip Collins, speechwriter, author and entrepreneur

'This book tells me so many things I wish I'd known before. Clear and witty, Chris Hirst brings his experience and insight to the task of leadership in a world changing at a startling pace. He is the ultimate No Bullsh*t Merchant'
John Kampfner, author of *Why the Germans Do It Better*

Praise for *No Bullsh*t Leadership*:

'A punchy, plainly written guide, offering a readable and enlightened view of what leaders do and how they should do it'   *Financial Times*

'A new rubric on leadership'   *Evening Standard*

'A brilliant set of leadership tools that will help you succeed whatever your goal'   Sir Clive Woodward

'Gets to the point of crucial leadership challenges in a simple and engaging way – it's rare to find a book that does this so beautifully. Yes, it's no bullshit, but it's also really elegant in its directness and uses beautiful stories to illustrate the points'
The Business Book Awards Judges

Chris Hirst has spent over a decade in CEO positions, including as Global CEO for Havas Creative Group. Once an engineering graduate working in a glass factory, his career path has taken him to the boardroom via Harvard Business School. Named in the *Evening Standard*'s Progress 1000 list and ranked one of the industry's most influential CEOs, Chris is a regular commentator in national and international press including *BBC News*, *The Politics Show*, the *Evening Standard*, *CNBC*, the *Financial Times* and *Sky News*. He also hosts the Intelligence Squared *No Bullsh*t Leadership* podcast. His book *No Bullsh*t Leadership* won Best Business Book of the Year 2020: Leadership for the Future, at the Business Book Awards. Visit his website www.chris-hirst.com for training, podcast, blogs and speaking. Follow him on Twitter @chrishirst.

No
Bullsh*t
Change

An 8 Step Guide
for Leaders

Chris Hirst

P

First published in Great Britain in 2023 by
Profile Books Ltd
29 Cloth Fair
London
EC1A 7JQ

www.profilebooks.com

1 3 5 7 9 10 8 6 4 2

Typeset by CC Book Production

Printed and bound in Great Britain by
Clays Ltd, Elcograf S.p.A.

A CIP catalogue record for this book is available from the British Library.

ISBN 978 1 80081 569 8
eISBN 978 1 80081 571 1

To Dad

CONTENTS

INTRODUCTION

To lead change, you must be able to achieve effective results in constantly changing environments, against unpredictable forces with imperfect information.

There is nothing more difficult to take in hand,
more perilous to conduct or more uncertain in its
success than to take the lead in the introduction
of a new order of things.

Niccolò Machiavelli

HOW SHOULD WE RESPOND when the unimaginable happens?

On 28 February 2020, I was in the back of a taxi in Mumbai on my way to speak at a conference. I was last on, a little nervous, and I'd had less time than usual to prepare. Habitually, in such a situation I would sit in silence and remind myself of the key points I wanted to hit, but this time I didn't have the opportunity. For the whole hour my companions and I talked breathlessly of a mysterious new disease that was racing across the world. Surely it couldn't be as serious as was claimed, or as contagious, or as difficult to contain. Surely it would come and go like so many other crises we'd known through our lives – storms that appeared on the horizon but blew quickly by. We drew comfort from familiarity – everything looked normal, nothing had changed, it would all be fine.

The conference came and went, as they do. The room

was large, windowless, airless and full. The hotel lobby teemed with people; the bar and buffet afterwards full of jostling delegates. From there we went straight to the packed airport terminal and hunted for seats in the lounge, all the while looking around with wide eyes – noticing, as if for the first time, the sheer enormity and proximity of humanity. Unbeknown to us, the tectonic plates had already split and rendered, the world irrevocably altered. The shock just hadn't reached us yet.

At whatever point in the future you read these words, one thing is for certain: never again will we unthinkingly assume that the near future, never mind the distant, will look mostly indistinguishable from the near past.

Leading change is the leader's ultimate test. During the pandemic we experienced the impact of those leaders able to rise to the challenge and the consequences of those who were not.

All leadership is about change, but in this book we will consider the specific circumstance when the fundamentals of the existing order are, or must be, upended. In this context, leading change is not, certainly not initially, a process of steady, measured progress, but should be considered little short of a revolution, approached with all the urgency, zeal and clarity that that description implies.

Successful change programmes are not, as often portrayed, activities pursued in splendid isolation like an academic exercise. To succeed, leaders must be able to achieve effective results in constantly changing environments, against unpredictable forces, with imperfect information. Many of the most significant factors a leader must contend with will be beyond their control, from macro-economic pressures and geo-politics to the responses of competitors and even sometimes employees. Leading change requires that leaders both respond effectively to those factors beyond their control and mould those that are within.

Dreadnoughts and valves

All leaders at some point will be faced with a circumstance where the methods, tools and thinking that had proved successful thus far can no longer be relied upon to succeed in the future. This point of inflexion is one of great challenge. For many, the greatest hurdle, at least initially, is in overcoming the cognitive dissonance of this circumstance: outwardly all may seem as it did yesterday, as it did last year, yet clouds gather on a horizon that had previously been sun-bleached blue. Perhaps, many silently hope, it will blow past.

In 1906, the Royal Navy launched one of the most revolutionary ships ever built, so much so that its very name, HMS *Dreadnought*, became synonymous with an entirely new breed of huge and awe-inspiring machine. The *Dreadnought* brought together for the first time an entire range of revolutionary technologies, from steam turbine engines to all-steel construction, and much more besides. However, her inception had posed a terrible dilemma for their Lordships of the Admiralty.

Only a year earlier, Britain had celebrated the hundredth

anniversary of the Battle of Trafalgar, where its most feted son, Admiral Nelson, had defeated a Napoleonic fleet, heralding a century of global dominance. Through the intervening years, the British had held on to their top-dog position through an uncomplicated, yet expensive expedient, one they called the 'two-power standard'. This dictated that they must maintain a naval fleet of a size at least as large as that of the next two biggest powers combined. By 1906, that was a lot of ships, and had cost a lot of money.

The *Dreadnought* represented a technological leap equivalent to that between propeller and jet. From the moment that King Edward VII smashed the wine bottle on its prow and the behemoth slid into Portsmouth Sound all existing battleships in the world were rendered obsolete. However, Britain's adversaries, though awed, were unlikely to be cowed.

Every action stimulates a reaction; every reaction demands a response. Their Lordships' dilemma had been that, though they may have moved first, where they trod others would surely race to follow. And the first consequence of their decisiveness? They now possessed more obsolete battleships than anybody else. HMS *Dreadnought* represented the start of a new era, and they had at that instant a total superiority over their opponents of just one.

The Admiralty, faced with the potential erosion of their position through technological change, opted for pre-emption, deciding that they must take control and act rather than allow external circumstances to dictate to them. If revolutionary change was coming, they reasoned, better to be in its vanguard than baggage car. Yet the decision, easy with hindsight, was far from it at the time. HMS *Dreadnought* represented the instantaneous erasure not simply of an old technology (wooden-sided, sail-powered fighting ships), but the entire training, staffing, procurement, strategy and fighting doctrine of the Royal Navy. The launch of the *Dreadnought* was nothing short of the end of Nelson's Royal Navy and the beginning of one entirely new, though with a consequently far less certain and pre-ordained future. Their Lordships, in their own way, had initiated a revolution, something that, in the ordinary run of affairs, cossetted in their Mayfair clubs, they very much frowned upon.

In the 1960s, electronic machines ran on valves. These look to us today a little like the oval lightbulbs found above the bars of modish Soho watering holes (New York or London – take your pick). The electronic valve industry was huge, but increasingly threatened by the new disruptive technology of the silicon transistor (which evolved into what we now know as the microchip). The leading valve manufacturers weren't dumb – far from it. Like the Royal Navy, they saw change coming, but reached a different conclusion. Rather than revolutionary change, they chose evolution. After all, they reasoned, embracing the transistor was a perilous, fraught and dangerous undertaking, one far from certain to succeed, and with unknowable future prospects. Such a pivot would erase all they had up to that point created.

In their chosen strategy, they were, by one measure, very successful. At the point where the entire industry disappeared (almost overnight) they were producing the smallest and fastest valves they'd ever made. Becoming better and better at what they had always done was a highway to oblivion. They were building fabulous sailing ships while the world wanted *Dreadnoughts*.

For leaders, the catalyst for change can be reactive, such as responding to the pandemic or technological innovation (the test faced and failed by the valve man-ufacturers). Or it can be proactive, a revolution of their own making, such as that instigated by the Royal Navy. More commonly it will be something of both push and pull. Ideally, as a leader you would be able to manage and control events, choose your own moment to act. Yet, as we know, the real world rarely affords such a luxury.

The need for change is often obvious with hindsight, but making the leap from status quo to reinvention is rarely easy. Many leaders find themselves in situations analogous to those discussed yet fail to grasp the urgency of the need. They are like the proverbial frog in warming water, failing to notice the incremental deterioration of their situation until it is too late. Or, more commonly, they see the signs but lack the clarity, determination or courage to act. The warming water is, after all, comfortable. Until the very end.

Those organisations that saw the danger but failed to act, or acted and failed anyway, are legion; many of them household names. In 2009, I worked with Nokia, then far and away the world's largest and most successful mobile phone manufacturer. It is easy now to forget that they were the poster child of the mobile revolution, a genu-inely loved and aspirational brand. In one meeting we raised with them the possible threat of the Apple iPhone (launched eighteen months earlier), then a super-premium product. Though Nokia had been one of the first to develop touchscreen technology, they dismissed the iPhone as a premium niche: 'we sell more handsets in a day than they do in a year,' they boasted. The internal inertia – cultural, contextual and financial – was just too great to overcome. What began as a failure of imagination ended as a failure of their business. By 2012, they faced bankruptcy.

Some examples we can consider in contrasting pairs. Blockbuster Video, once on every British high street, rented out its final DVD in 2010, yet a close contemporary, Netflix, shifted from postal DVD delivery to online delivery and ultimately to the vanguard of a global revolution in not simply content distribution (where, like Blockbuster, they began) but creation. For Blockbuster, read valves; for Netflix, *Dreadnoughts*.

Failure to act guarantees failure

These and many others are examples not of businesses that failed because their product or brand was poor – in many cases they remain, even today, very well-known. They failed because, though they saw the threat, they were unable or unwilling to act.

Leaders in all roles and at all levels are assailed from without and within by reasons (often good reasons) why they should do nothing, to stick with the status quo, the most compelling often being the risk and uncertainty that change inevitably brings. However, the surest guarantee of failure is the failure to act; their faltering first steps foreshadow their eventual defeat.

Too many leaders never really begin at all. They meet the fork in the path and choose that which is more familiar and seemingly safer. Many tell themselves that of course change is needed, just not today. They opt instead for what they know – to make better and better valves, or faster and faster sailing ships.

All leaders, at one time or another, find themselves at this point of inflexion: status quo or revolution.

Status quo because most of what you have done and known in the past will continue to serve you well into the medium future. For all leaders, most of their time is spent here. Nobody, no matter what they claim in their TED Talks, can exist in a state of permanent revolutionary change.

Revolution because sometimes a slightly better, faster, smaller version of the status quo won't do. Because the behaviours, culture, process and thinking that have served to this point are no longer fit for purpose. Revolution because your greatest certainty is simply that the past can no longer serve as your guide. All leaders must at one time or another face up to this sometimes startling reality. Leading change is their greatest and yet most rewarding test.

Overcoming the warm inertia of the status quo is the leader's first battle. Leadership is primarily the act of influencing the behaviour and performance of others, but leading change begins with you. First, you must be convinced of the need to change. Hesitation is understandable, impulsivity to be resisted.

The consequent demand for those who can effect meaningful change has never been greater. The best, and the teams or organisations they lead, will grasp these opportunities rather than wilt before them. This ability, in an ever-shifting world, to steer your own course is the ultimate route to personal and professional fulfilment and, dare I say, happiness.

A story of change

For the past fifteen years I have been responsible for leading, advising and ultimately transforming hundreds of businesses, big and small, on every continent. In 2019, I wrote a book about what I'd learnt.

In the early part of the century, I was hired as part of a new change management team tasked with turning round a dull, dying business, by general consensus considered unfixable. I was the Managing Director, No. 2 to the CEO. He was the brightest and most exciting star of his generation. I and my new colleagues considered ourselves to be an unbeatable team, reassured by our collective expertise, experience and confidence. The business may be unfixable, but we knew we couldn't fail. Except we did.

Within six months the CEO who had hired us had gone. Within twelve months the new team had begun to shatter, and by twenty-four months there were few of us left. Over the next four years new CEOs came and went, but the business stayed stubbornly unchanged, its gradual decline unabated. By 2009, after six years as Managing Director, once part of the solution, I had become part of the problem. I believed, with good reason, that I had screwed my once promising career. It had been a salutary and painful lesson, a case study in how not to do it. How simply being talented isn't enough. How nemesis follows hubris.

At length and perhaps somewhat too late, I decided that I must take my future into my own hands. If I was no longer part of the solution, then I would have to start afresh. It almost didn't matter where; perhaps I would leave the industry altogether. It was a scary prospect. By now I had a young family, a mortgage and all the other responsibilities that freight our decisions and incentivise inertia.

Then, suddenly, a piece of luck. I found myself with a new boss, who unexpectedly offered me the opportunity to take charge. The question was, could I take it? After six years of failure, could we fix the unfixable?

I found myself as CEO with little thought of what the role demanded. However, I was determined of one thing above all others: that I would make the best possible use of the one resource I had – my six years of failure. I had seen first-hand how to fail at the task that now lay before me. From this I drew three important lessons that would provide the energy to fuel our new beginning:

1. Leading change is a team sport

I couldn't do it alone. We needed a close team at the top if we wanted to build a high-performing organisation.

2. Sometimes, revolution is the only way
The scale of the challenge we faced demanded an iconoclastic approach. We resolved there would be no sacred cows in our reinvention of the organisation.

And, most importantly,

3. Success is a consequence of learning from failure
We may not have been clear exactly how we were going to go about our task, but we were certain what we were *not* going to do. We were not going to repeat the mistakes we and others had made over the preceding six years. If mistakes were going to be made (and they inevitably were), we were going to make new ones, all of our own.

So began my own personal journey of change.

Within three years we had gone from being a dog of a business to one of the hottest in the world. What follows is the distillation of the lessons I learnt during the dark years of failure and bright years of success, and what I have learnt since leading change programmes for businesses around the world.

No bullsh*t change

You're here because something's wrong, broken or slowing down. Things just don't quite feel right; dark clouds are gathering on the horizon. And you're here because you're going to fix it. In this eight-module programme, broken into respective chapters, I intend to give you the confidence, the clarity and the tools to do just that.

This then is a manual to allow you to effect rapid and lasting change, whatever your circumstance – whether leading a team of six or a multinational of sixty thousand, a government department or a mid-table sports team, a shop floor or a showroom. The principles of leading successful change programmes are universal.

In writing this book, my objective is two-fold: clarity and action. Though I have organised my ideas in a deliberate order, one that I believe makes for most ready comprehension and utility, their real-world application will necessarily be more fluid. Consider leading change as the gradual illumination of a darkened room. As each subsequent row of lights are switched on, the effect is cumulative, but the order in which you switch them on matters less than that they are all eventually lit. And of course, if they begin to go out again, darkness returns as quickly as it retreated. It's your task not simply to switch them on, but to keep them alight.

All change must begin with an honest understanding of your current context. In **Chapter 1, 'Baseline', we explore how to understand the situation you find yourself in today and use that to overcome the internal inertia that resists change**. It's not difficult, but it's very important.

In **Chapter 2 we look at why effective communication is so important when leading change**. We will consider some common (and easily avoided) mistakes and introduce a straightforward and universally applicable guide to doing it well.

Objective-setting is often misunderstood, unnecessarily overcomplicated, ineffective and even self-defeating. Yet a clear objective is essential to any change programme. In **Chapter 3 we explore how to define effective objectives**, why it's not as difficult as we are often told, how to use them for maximum effect and why they are critical for building effective teams.

The most difficult part of any change programme is the start. Your greatest challenge is often not that people don't believe change would be desirable, but that they don't believe it is ever going to happen. In **Chapter 4, 'Breaking Free', we learn why urgency and energy are critical to getting started**, help you build credibility as an action-oriented change-leader, and most importantly build confidence that your programme can and will succeed.

Chapter 5 considers the importance of teams and coalitions and why the more great leaders you have, the quicker you'll achieve your goals.

We are all good at being able to see the things that are broken, dysfunctional or could be improved. However, attempting to tackle everything at once will only guarantee failure. **Chapter 6 introduces the concept of *Schwerpunkt*, the point of maximum effort** (you don't need to be able to pronounce it, just understand it) as a means of focusing your effort, and how this will accelerate you towards your goal.

Chapter 7 explains why, ultimately, all organisational change is culture change. It is also a no bullshit primer on what culture is, why it matters and how to build the effective and enduring culture you need in order to succeed.

Finally, in **Chapter 8 we arrive at the end of the beginning**. Most change programmes consider what is in reality only the start, but in the real world, effective change demands consistent effort, a great deal of determination and a willingness to learn from failure. Change doesn't happen in isolation, but is a contingent process that must adapt as it progresses.

This programme is designed to be a tool to help you lead effective change from the smallest team to the largest organisation. It is intended to inspire, inform and, most importantly, enable. The steps, tools and examples are not formed from simple academic study, but rather decades of practical experience – from great victories and crushing, tears-in-the-eyes defeats.

I don't present this programme as the only way, but recommend it to you as a proven way. You wouldn't learn to fly from someone who had never left the ground, and nor should you learn to lead change from those who have never walked in your shoes. In leading change, the best you can hope for is intelligent, but imperfect progress. And if in doubt, do.

1

BASELINE

You can't fix something if you don't understand
what it is you're trying to fix.

You can't lead change if you haven't made a compelling case
for why change is needed.

You can't use an old map to explore a new world.
Albert Einstein

The first principle is that you must not fool yourself,
and you are the easiest person to fool.
Richard Feynman

IN 1783, NEVIL MASKELYNE, the Astronomer Royal, received an inflammatory letter. In it the author claimed that Greenwich, the site of the Royal Observatory, wasn't where Maskelyne thought it was, that its latitude and longitude had been calculated incorrectly. Worse still, it had been sent by Cassini de Thury, of all horrors, a Frenchman.

The French had recently completed a revolutionary map of the then (but not for much longer) Kingdom of France. It was the first map to be produced on modern scientific lines using the latest technology, geodesic triangulation, delivering a degree of accuracy that would be recognisable even today. Nothing like it existed *outre-Manche*, and Maskelyne, though dismissive of the criticism, smelt opportunity. Using the pretext of the letter, he rapidly obtained government funding for a British version of just such a project.

Today we think little of maps. GPS allows us to know precisely where we are at all times. However, accurate maps changed the world. The problem is, before it is possible to create such a map, you must know with great certainty where you are starting from. Thus, De Thury's message was more than simply a passing swipe at the accuracy of English measurement, it was a warning that not only did they lack an accurate map of the kingdom, but they were in no position to create one.

So began the first modern survey of the whole of Great Britain and Ireland, a project that took fully sixty-two years to complete, yet one that stood the test of time, only being fully revised in the mid-twentieth century.

Triangulation is, as its name suggests, a model of mapping based on the specific geometric properties of a triangle, and the division of the territory to be mapped into accurately measured versions of the same. The greater the accuracy of each triangle's measurements, the greater the accuracy of the maps produced. The distinctive white 'trig points' still to be found dotted across the British landscape were the original reference points chosen for the corners of these triangles.

The first task of any such survey is to establish a base-line, the point from which all other calculations will be made and the first side of the first triangle, and this foundational work was undertaken by the Scottish military engineer Major-General William Roy. A site was chosen, one end of which is located on what is today a perimeter road of Heathrow airport. These first measurements were taken with painstaking care, using twenty-foot glass rods in 1,370 individual stages, each of which was required to be accurate to within a thousandth of an inch. Only once this baseline was complete could mapping begin.

The importance of a baseline

Maps help us determine how we might get to our future destination, but as anybody who has attempted to use one will know, their first and most important task is to tell you where you already are.

To lead change you need a baseline. This is the foundation on which your future actions will be built. It performs two critical roles that we will consider in this and the following chapter.

1. **It is an accurate and universal understanding of where you are to begin** – specifically, the current status of the organisation and its challenges, be they internal, external or, most commonly, a mix of the two.

2. **It forms the basis from which you build alignment amongst all your relevant stakeholders**. Within many organisations there is a widespread (if incomplete) understanding of its problems – problems that multiply the longer they are left unattended. The baseline is a critical step in building a powerful and aligned coalition that will support the actions required to achieve your goal. Without this alignment progress will be difficult, if not impossible.

If it's broke, first understand it

All successful change begins with a clear and accurate description of the situation that you and your team find yourselves in today. This is your baseline. Mostly, unlike that faced by Major-General Roy and his thermally sensitive glass rods, this is not a difficult question to answer. It is, however, like his, an important one. You can't fix something if you don't know what it is you're trying to fix. You can't improve a system that you don't fully understand. Perhaps most importantly, you can't lead change if you haven't made a compelling case for why change is needed.

Internal and external context

When drawing up the baseline, there are two broad areas to consider and understand. Either, or both, of these may provide the motive force for change. They are:

1. **External context**
This includes such things as the macro-economic environment (as a consequence of the pandemic, for example), geopolitics (Brexit or the Ukraine war), competitor activity (pricing or product innovation) and legislative change (such as GDPR). This is not an exhaustive list, but it's a good snapshot of the multitude of factors a leader must contend with that are largely or wholly beyond their control.

2. **Internal context**
This includes everything from product quality, new

product development, marketing, production processes, structure and workflow to culture, pricing,
employee relations, talent retention and talent attraction. Again, not an exhaustive list, but a good cross
section of the areas that are mostly or wholly within
a leader's control. At least in theory.

It's obvious, but important to remember, that even if
external factors are the driver of your organisation's need
to change, **only those within your control are available
to you to try and fix it**.

The challenges of being an insider

The process of understanding your baseline is one that
most obviously applies to someone new to an organisation, team or department. However, in the majority of
situations, change is led by leaders who are already in
place.

As an incumbent, you too must be able to define and
communicate your baseline. Indeed, it could be argued
that by being an insider, the processes of baseline setting is even more important and potentially difficult, as
much of what must be changed may have been instigated
or maintained by you. Consequently, incumbent leaders
typically face two challenges.

The first is that they view the process as threatening –
an unwanted referendum on their performance. This logic
is understandable, but flawed; you must, as far as is possible, control the impulses of your ego. If you are going

to fix something, you have to understand it, and that applies whether you're newly appointed to the position or not. If you are the incumbent and you don't fix it, it's a reasonable assumption that sooner or later somebody else will be asked to try. This can be a threatening, but also liberating realisation; action, as always, is your most certain route to success. A common cause of leadership failure is the unwillingness to recognise that what has worked in the past will no longer work in the future.

Secondly, a leader must by definition be part of the solution, not part of the problem. A regular and objective re-evaluation of the baseline is critical to ensuring that this is the case – one that is performed, as far as is possible, without preconception or precondition. For a change-focused leader this isn't a process that happens to you, but one you lead, learn from and use as the basis for the next actions you must take. You have to be prepared to challenge the assumptions that have served you well to this point, and in establishing your baseline be willing to confront and, if necessary, overturn existing patterns, habits and beliefs – including your own. Perhaps especially your own. Easier said than done, but that is what change entails.

All successful leaders must be prepared to conduct objective, periodic reappraisals of their organisation's performance, objectives and strategy – to shed their team's skin and start again. In fact if they don't, they risk being replaced by someone who will. Very often the first act of a change programme is to replace the leader, because those in post are unable or unwilling to act.

One of this book's primary ambitions is to stop this being you.

Symptoms and diagnosis

Symptoms are easy to see; diagnosis can be less straight-forward. Horror films make great play on this, and their protagonists' initial naïvety. The four teenagers in an isolated lodge for a birthday weekend assume the strange noises in the night must just be owls, or bears or the wind. So confident are they that the least famous actor wanders off to check it out. Blood, gore and screaming ensue. In *Aliens*, the jock space marines scoff at the Cassandra-like Ripley and, muscles bulging, head out to swat the bugs beneath the nuclear power plant. Blood, gore and screaming ensue. In each case they see the symptoms but, fatally for the minor characters, misdiagnose the source.

Commonly in all organisations, problems are similarly easy to spot. However, new and incumbent leaders have almost directly opposing challenges in deciding their course of action. Incumbent leaders must beware the assumption that what has always worked in the past will continue to work in the future – and not ignore the flashing red lights on the dashboard until it is too late (certainly too late for them). And in contrast, it is common for new leaders to simply damn all that went before and set about slinging the baby out with the bathwater. In both instances a clear and well-defined baseline would save an awful lot of trouble, heartache and, perhaps in some instances, blood, gore and screaming.

A decline in sales, for example, is an obvious, and a clear red flag for any organisation. But finding out why is often more difficult and, despite the siren voices you may hear, can rarely be attributed to one cause alone. Some may be convinced that it's all because your pesky, bigger, more ruthless, better-funded competitor has dropped their prices. It is certainly always tempting to blame your woes on others. But might it also be because the cachet that once surrounded your brand, and for which your loyal customers were willing to pay a premium, has faded? A rather more subtle, difficult and potentially unpopular message to deliver, not least because for this you can blame nobody but yourselves. However, what may initially be unpopular (specifically the discovery that the problem is predominantly your fault) may in fact be good news. If it's you that has gone astray, then it is wholly within your gift to fix it. All you now have to do is work out how.

Understanding is the prelude to solving

When storm clouds gather, it is tempting yet potentially fatal to simply blame others. And though external factors are real, they are also, by definition, beyond your control. If your big, ruthless competitor has copied your marketing, hired your head of R&D and cut their prices, what are you going to do about it? Feeling sorry for yourself and moaning about them in the pub will achieve nothing. You must be brutally honest about the problems you face and realistic when considering the factors you *can* control. Only then can you begin to find a solution.

We live in a world of growing polarisation. Our problems multiply; we damn those with whom we disagree rather than seeking to understand. Compromise is increasingly portrayed as weak, uncaring or worse. But understanding is not agreeing. Understanding is the prelude to solving. This is why a clear baseline is of such fundamental importance. Without a thorough understanding of a problem it cannot be solved, and understanding very often requires the finding and sharing of uncomfortable truths. As Nevil Maskelyne discovered.

Your first job is to ask lots of questions and, most importantly, to listen carefully to what you're told, whether you're new to the role or not.

The perils of confirmation bias

In reaching understanding, the effective collection and interpretation of data is critical. Done well, it can be the cornerstone of your thinking. However, it is no panacea. Data is simply another tool and, as with any tool, only as effective as those who use it. Throughout the Covid pandemic, we became all too familiar with how two equally well-intentioned and qualified experts can look at the same data and draw very different conclusions. And, of course, how others carefully sifted through the findings to cherry-pick those points that supported their existing views.

Confirmation bias is the tendency to search for, prioritise or favour information that supports our existing views or opinions. We all suffer from it. It causes us to give undue weight to certain sources of information and downplay or ignore others. It is no minor factor to be acknowledged and forgotten. It is a powerful force, capable of shaping the very fundamentals of our beliefs and behaviour, sometimes leading even the most experienced astray.

In 1955, in one of his final acts, Albert Einstein wrote an effusive foreword for a book called *Earth's Shifting Crust: A Key to Some Basic Problems of Earth Science*. Written by an eminent geologist named Charles Hapgood, the book aimed to demolish what the author saw as a crazy, even heretical, idea that had begun to gain traction – an idea we now call plate tectonics. First posited in 1908 by an amateur American geologist, Frank Bursley Taylor, it was dismissed immediately by almost the entirety of the scientific community as self-evidently ridiculous: how could continents move?

In writing his book nearly half a century later, Hapgood considered it an idea he must kill off once and for all. Some gullible and excitable souls, he observed, thankfully little more than a noisy minority, had noticed 'an apparent correspondence in shape between certain continents ... that South America might be fitted together with Africa, and so on'. He reassured his readers that extensive research, as well of course as centuries of received wisdom, showed the notion to be groundless. Well into the 1970s, influential geological textbooks continued to dismiss plate tectonics as a physical impossibility.

It is a seductive fallacy to dismiss Hapgood as a fool; he was anything but. Lest we forget, the century's greatest mind had endorsed his work. Rather, he saw only the evaporating pool of evidence that supported the orthodoxy and was blind to the, by then, huge and growing lake of that which did not.

Confirmation bias is a powerful force indeed, often, as in the example above, driven by vested interest, ego and status as much as innocent misinterpretation. Consequently, although research, statistics and modelling have the potential to bring great insight and understanding, they often unintentionally end up being used simply to reinforce or support the status quo.

It is visible everywhere (if we look for it). The media love 'research', but isn't it strange how the research produced always appears to support and endorse the views of the people who paid for it? Wouldn't it be refreshing to read a headline that ran, 'We've done some research and we were wrong, says expert.' It doesn't often happen.

We all have biases and, in the context of research and data, confirmation bias is possibly the most pervasive. It's not the evidence that's wrong, it's our unwillingness or inability to use it effectively that is at fault. It takes a brave and open-minded person to accept the overturning of their long-held beliefs, irrespective of how strong the evidence is. Therefore, when defining your baseline you must ensure you aren't simply seeing what you want to see. Or being told what people think you want to hear.

A great example is customer feedback. Perhaps you have surveyed a major customer and with relief see that the CEO has given you a very positive response – naturally, the response you want. You glance quickly down the list and note that some of the other people on her team appear to be far less complimentary, but you've got the headline: the person at the top is happy. Move on. This is dangerous, and is the cause of many fractured relationships and, ultimately, lost customers. The reasons are obvious and legion: the CEO may leave, she may not be the main day-to-day contact, she may actually be interested in what the rest of her team think, and so on. Like so much else, it's obvious when written down, but it's a mistake we've all made.

Another might be feedback on a team member. The collection of data for performance reviews is time-consuming and consequently often a hurried task. No judgement here, it's just how it is.

In our thought experiment we collect five pieces of feedback on Freya, four of which align with each other and one that takes a contrary point of view. Though a qualitative exercise, the temptation is to treat it as quantitative. Furthermore, do we simply align with the opinions (whether those in the majority or minority) that fit with our own? Many do.

Of course, if we want our feedback to be effective in helping Freya progress, the correct answer is none of the above. We need to use the responses as a tool that helps us to help her. But it takes time, thought and, in this example, further work to be able to do so effectively.

As an aside, simplistic example though this is, it is typical of how 360-degree feedback often operates in practice, and it is the failure (often through lack of time and judicious application of confirmation biases) to get beneath the headline data that makes so many such programmes little more than box-ticking exercises and, consequently, missed opportunities.

Selecting the data that matters most

A baseline provides a universally understood definition of the foundations upon which you will build. It is an individualised snapshot in time, one that will be specific to the circumstances your team faces. There can, by definition, be no generalised answers. All football teams play by identical rules under all but identical circumstances. However, two teams locked together at the top of the league may find themselves with completely different baselines: one may have the challenge that they let in too many goals, the other that they fail to score often enough. To achieve their ultimate objective they must clearly understand not simply the symptom but the specific underlying problem.

The interdependence between baseline and objective

Now that we have considered the importance of a carefully constructed baseline, we will next consider how to find it, free, as far as possible, of our preconceptions, biases and (dare I say) insecurities.

Electrons are complicated and counter-intuitive things. One of their many mind-bending tricks is that they are able to be in two places at once. (In fact they can be in an infinite amount of places at once, but let's not go there right now.) When considering your baseline, it is useful to learn a little from my simplified electron in order to clarify and simplify your task.

All organisations collect data, lots of it, all of the time. Customer data, sales data, financial data, viewing data, website visits, employee data – the list is all but endless and the volume continues to climb. However, the simple act of collecting data is no guarantee that you or anybody else is learning anything useful from it. Indeed, for many organisations the sheer amount of data collected is in itself a barrier to its effective use. Even in small teams leaders can become overwhelmed. A key choice leaders need to make is to decide, of all the data that is available, which is most useful in determining their baseline. One way to do so is to imagine yourself like the electron, in two places at once – at both the start and the end of your journey.

A baseline is a means to an end. And if it is a means to an end, it is useful to have some idea of what your end might be. Though change is non-linear, books generally are and we will explore the setting of effective objectives in more detail in Chapter 3. Nevertheless, in the real world your baseline and objective are two points on the same journey. A sketched outline of your likely desired destination is therefore one of the most powerful ways to understand what data inputs will be most useful when defining your beginning.

You need to be able to look forward to describe a motivating and exciting future, but you also need to be able to imagine looking backward from that future to today in order to help decide, of all the data points you might choose, which will be most helpful in describing the initial nature of your task.

This interdependence between beginning and end is why change is best understood as a series of loops, something we will explore in more detail in Chapter 8. The initial definition of your objective is likely to be imperfect, but it is equally unlikely to be completely inaccurate; you'll refine it as you progress. Similarly, and inevitably, the ways you define your baseline will come into sharper focus as you learn, develop and advance.

In order to cut through the data clutter and be able to focus on what will be most useful for the journey ahead, be more like an electron and imagine yourself in two places at once.

Sharing builds comprehension, engagement and alignment

Though organisations collect a huge amount of data, they are often reluctant to share it. This is an example of a phenomenon common in organisations of all types: the infantilisation of their employees. This stems from a wrong-headed and patronising belief that the majority would not be interested in, able to understand or would even be made anxious by the widespread sharing of key performance metrics.

Nothing could be further from the truth. The leader should encourage widespread sharing of key data points – both the good and the bad. She will be given a multitude of reasons for not doing so. A common one is the fear of leaks to competitors, which, though valid in some circumstances, is neither insurmountable nor usually good enough a reason to outweigh the benefits of the whole team being clear about the exact status of the wider organisation and therefore being better able to improve their own personal contribution: your ultimate objective.

In my experience, there is very little important data that cannot be widely shared within an organisation, and yet commonly the reality is the opposite. Often I have sat in leadership meetings discussing the fact that many of our people don't understand how we make money (yes really), and debating whether we should share how much money we are or aren't making (yes really) – truly the most basic of all data points. It sounds so crazy written down that I deleted and replaced that sentence several times. It stays in because if it is true for me, it is true for many others also. And if it is a problem for the teams I have been responsible for, it is also a problem for others.

That all but the most sensitive information *can* be shared is not to say that it *should* be shared. Simply blocking up people's emails won't help comprehension, but effective sharing of metrics that tell a clear story are an important part of widening understanding of your baseline position and building your coalition. Organisations don't function well if department boundaries are impermeable, and the sharing of status and progress are a powerful way to engage everybody in the tasks that matter rather than those that simply sit within their perimeter.

What gets measured gets done; what gets shared gets attention

I have frequently used the deliberate business-wide sharing of key performance indicators (KPIs) as a driver of baseline comprehension and, ultimately, of course, of change. In a recent role we identified five data points that we considered to be the most significant in measuring our progress (in addition to financial performance). They were:

- Employee engagement
- Customer satisfaction
- New customer acquisition
- Diversity, equity and inclusion (DE&I) – in our case we identified a number of key metrics around the ethnic and gender composition of our employee base in addition to pay gap analysis
- Environmental impact.

We shared these widely and included them in all business planning sessions. They provided both an initial baseline and milestones to measure progress. Like my imaginary electron, our end point helped define our start.

There are many organisations for whom similar metrics would work, but it's not only the measuring that matters. It's what you do with them: how you share them; how you bake them into individual objectives; how you define individual responsibilities as a consequence; how you use them to troubleshoot and to continually refine your strategies and next steps. As we progressed we learnt and evolved what we measured. A key task is to find the right metrics for you.

Data means little, without action

The effective dissemination and discussion of data should become a cultural totem. Debriefs should not be simply events that are awaited with fingers crossed and then forgotten until next time, but rather opportunities to share learning, best practice and to refine strategies for improvement. Across the various businesses I have led and worked with, we see a clear correlation between those that are smart and inventive about how they manage the dissemination of data and their ability to learn and grow.

It's so obvious, I question myself in writing it down. However, obvious though it may be, occasions where the careful collection of accurate and useful data has made absolutely no difference whatsoever to the performance of a team are commonplace. The data arrives, but is regarded much as a poor yachtsman might regard the wind: it would be wonderful if it would go in the right direction, but until it chooses to we must drift along as best we can. For an effective leader at any level, all forms of business or organisational insight are merely the prelude to action. As we will see in a later chapter, clarity counts for nothing without action.

Effective sharing and discussion helps ensure that

everyone is focused on the same ultimate goals, spurs teams into action through the positive example of others and aids problem-solving, as it is common for different teams to be confronted with similar challenges, for example, a poor customer relationship. Meetings such as these create opportunities for serendipity that simply would not happen were the data kept siloed, quiet and private. It genuinely is true that great ideas can come from anywhere and if everybody is invested in, and aware of, the numbers that matter, they are all more likely to focus on the personal actions they can take to help.

Having defined the data points that matter most to your baseline, set about sharing as much of those as you can.

Three simple principles for effective dissemination of data:

1. Remember why you're sharing it

People's inboxes and diaries are already full, so be sparing and focused. In this instance your objective is to build comprehension of your baseline, alignment around the shared task at hand and cross-pollination of ideas, so consider what data best lands those points and what collective forums will have the most effect.

2. Over-communicate: fewer facts, but more often

People can only remember so much, so say less, but more often.

3. Explain why

A previous boss of mine once said to me when preparing a presentation to her biggest client: he likes his food predigested, so do the work for him.

It's a great rule of thumb here and elsewhere. Make what you share easy to understand, help people draw the relevant conclusions and, as far as possible, spell out the actions you and they should take.

Qualitative research: two-way focus groups

Though numbers tell stories, they rarely tell you all. Data, though powerful, makes it easy to forget that change, at heart, is an activity concerned with behaviours: persuading people, sometimes lots of people, to do things differently. Formal or informal focus groups put your people at the centre. There are a multitude of ways they can be used and, though for clarity I have treated them here primarily as an internal tool, you should use them with whichever audiences best help you achieve your objectives. Used well they are a very powerful and effective way to get deep insight into the nature of an organisation and its challenges.

Qualitative research provides you with an opportunity to both listen and communicate with your most important stakeholders, always a clarifying experience. And, like much else, though glaringly obvious, it is often forgotten.

However, this is a book about change, not research, and we are interested in how we can use these sessions in a way that will move us most effectively towards our goal. I therefore propose that the groups you run are treated as a two-way process.

In nearly every change programme I have run I have used this variation of qualitative research. They can simultaneously fulfil three critical objectives:

1. Learning
This is what all well-run focus groups do. They add a much-needed human dimension to inform the development of your baseline.

Note: Given the necessarily fluid nature of leading through change, focus groups can be used at any stage throughout your journey, and there will certainly be future occasions when they will again be useful. Indeed, you may decide to make them a fixed feature of the culture.

2. Sharing
Qualitative interactions provide an opportunity to gain feedback on what you've learnt and, as your journey progresses, to help refine your thinking. Be open and inclusive. Share, question and listen. Sense-check your assumptions and road-test hypotheses.

At their best, they are not simply opportunities to get feedback on what you've done, but a powerful way to get new and different voices from outside your bubble (more to come on that in a moment) to actively shape your thinking.

3. Collective ownership

Perhaps the most overlooked and important role they can play is in achieving buy-in to your project. Change isn't about you, it's about everybody else (certainly everybody else in the teams you are responsible for), and to succeed your baseline must ultimately be everybody's baseline, your objective everybody's objective.

Run well, these groups allow you the chance to build and develop your coalition for change and to begin the process of sharing ownership of what began as your project. In the long run, if it remains only yours, you will fail.

It is important to emphasise that in order to fulfil their potential these three objectives must be clear upfront, both to those running the sessions and to those taking part. Effective preparation and clarity of objectives will make for great and powerful sessions that can form a cornerstone of your programme throughout.

All the light you cannot see: uncovering what's hidden

This final section is perhaps the most important, most frequently overlooked and most difficult.

A feature of healthy cultures is that people feel able to be open and honest with one another. In many organisations this is not the case. Furthermore, you would be well advised not to casually assume this doesn't apply to yours.

Organisations need hierarchies in order to function well, but hierarchies also create barriers that can make it difficult for leaders to get a true sense of what is happening. In 1787, Grigory Potemkin built a series of fake villages to line the route of Empress Catherine II as she travelled from Moscow to the Crimea to show the apparent health and wealth of the country. The villages were disassembled after she had passed and reassembled at her next planned stop. Like the infamous Potemkin attempting to win the Empress's favour, in poor cultures people up and down the hierarchy judge it personally beneficial to avoid telling inconvenient truths. Consequently, for many leaders, existing or new, much of what is really happening in the organisation is hidden from them; they don't know what they don't know.

The higher up in the hierarchy you are, the more important it is for you to be sure people are telling you what you need to hear and not what they think you want to hear: that they disagree; that they have a new solution; that all is not as it should be; that the biggest customer is unhappy; that they have a problem they need help fixing. But too often, this is not our experience. We find ourselves unknowingly in a bubble. Or perhaps we do know, but quite like it; they are, after all, nice, comfortable places to be.

In your bubble, everybody seems to agree with you, laughs at your jokes and nods at all your ideas. The problem is, this isn't real. And, whisper it, they might not really agree, and may not actually find you funny. Culture, it is sometimes said, is what happens when you're not in the room.

If you want to know what's really happening you need to be prepared to see things, hear things and be told things that you might not want to hear. However, not hearing them doesn't mean they aren't being said, or done, or not done, and if you want to create a revolution you have to know where to start.

For some leaders, geography can be a key driver of separation and dislocation. The executive floor with its plush carpets and Aesop scents is alive and thriving in many organisations. But beware – even if you sit in amongst your team, that doesn't necessarily mean you are hearing all you need to hear.

Cutting through the hierarchy

It is amazing what you learn when you leave your desk and the effect it can have on the people you find yourself talking to as a result. Perhaps if Empress Catherine had spoken to one of the villagers she would have discovered they were actors – although members of the Russian nobility didn't do a lot of pressing the flesh.

I recently asked General Sir Chris Deverell, a former member of the British Army's Chiefs of Staff, how he dealt with this problem in an organisation as stratified as the army. How, I wondered, did he find out what was really going on and in turn make sure his messages were cutting through?

'I did it myself,' he told me. 'I think a leader of today cannot rely on hierarchical message delivery … you also have to find ways of taking in information that is not dependent on that hierarchy. There were too many rungs in that ladder, too many possibilities for people who didn't agree with me not communicating my message ... I felt very strongly that I needed to communicate direct to what you might call the workforce. And to that end, I did a lot of visiting units, and town halls where you stand up and deliver your message.'

The post-pandemic rise in remote and hybrid working has exacerbated this problem. Though hybrid working can be a win-win for employer and employee, it means leaders run the risk of being even more disconnected from different voices and different opinions. Modern technology and its promise of greater connectivity has instead had the effect of disconnecting more and more leaders from their teams. An email is not the same as a phone call, a Zoom call not the same as meeting face to face, and the kind of connection you make in a meeting not the same as a chat over dinner. All have their place, but too often we end up defaulting to the medium that is most convenient rather than most effective.

A culture that facilitates the effective sharing of ideas and information should be a priority for all leaders. Hierarchy matters, but it can't be allowed to become an impermeable barrier. You and your leaders need to go out of your way to ensure you regularly hear a range of different voices, opinions, ideas and even criticisms. Some organisations institute forums, surgeries or meetings that are deliberately constructed with this in mind. At BBC Radio 1, they used to call these meetings pizza meetings (because they provided free food); at Pixar they call them Braintrust meetings. It's obvious when said out loud, but so often isn't done. If you don't provide opportunities for light to be shone into even the darkest corners, what is hidden will remain hidden.

The most important thing with bubbles is to be aware that they exist. You can't fully escape, but self-awareness gives you the opportunity to get beyond them at least some of the time. And beware, the less visible or aware you are of your bubble, the thicker its walls.

So set about getting out.

Now write it down

Your baseline is not only for you – in fact it may not even primarily be for you – but it is a critical tool.

Your baseline describes your challenge and is the basis for building the case for change among your relevant stakeholders (who we will meet in the next chapter).

It also identifies a key set of metrics that act as markers along your route. They should be shared as widely as possible and updated regularly. This ensures that your entire team or organisation are clear on what areas matter most and, crucially, that they too can see and feel the progress you are making.

NO BULLSH*T BASELINE

You can't fix something if you don't know what it is you're trying to fix.
You can't lead change if you haven't made a compelling case
for why change is needed.

Clarity and accuracy are key

Change begins with a clear and accurate description of the situation
that you and your team find yourselves in today.
This is your baseline, the foundation on which your future actions
will be built.

Why your baseline is so important

1. Without a thorough understanding of a problem it cannot be
   solved.
2. It is a powerful tool when building alignment with key stakeholders.

Beware confirmation bias

Be sure you aren't simply seeing what you want to see – or being
told what people think you want to hear.

Uncover what is hidden

In poor cultures people avoid telling inconvenient truths. Consequently, for many leaders, much of what is really happening in the
organisation is hidden from them.

Hierarchy cannot be an impermeable barrier

If necessary, create forums and opportunities to cut through the layers of the organisation.

The collection and interpretation of data is no panacea

It is a tool, and only as effective as those who use it.

Share what you learn

Effective and frequent sharing of what you learn is critical in building widespread comprehension and engagement with your project, and alignment with your stakeholders.

Principles for dissemination of information

Be selective.
What gets measured gets done; what gets shared gets attention.
Over-communicate – fewer facts, but more often.
Explain why – predigest the meal.

Write it down; share it widely

Write down what you learn, identify key metrics to measure and shape your route, and share it widely and frequently.

2

COMMUNICATION

Communication is critical to success. In order to succeed,
effective and frequent communication is required of you and
those around you at every stage. Take care to do it well.

Communicate, communicate, communicate.
General Sir Chris Deverell

In teamwork, silence isn't golden, it's deadly.
Mark Sanborn

THE MAJORITY OF THIS BOOK'S most important topics can be divided into self-contained modules: Baseline, Objective and so on. There are two, however, that must instead be considered as *leitmotifs*, in that they run throughout. These are Communication (Chapter 2), which we will cover now, and Culture (Chapter 7).

Both Communication and Culture are indispensable considerations at all stages of your change programme. It is impossible to lead without consistent, effective communication; likewise, it is impossible to build effective teams without an understanding of the power and constraints of their cultural context.

In the interests of clarity, I have decided to treat Communication and Culture as stand-alone chapters even though neither can ever be considered wholly in isolation. Though a degree of repetition is therefore inevitable and necessary, I hope by this approach to keep it to a minimum.

At the time of writing, Russia's nihilistic war in Ukraine grinds on. Horrific though it is, it has given us an inspiring and enduring leadership icon in Volodymyr Zelensky. If ever there was a case of cometh the hour, cometh the man, it is he. Zelensky was initially dismissed as literally a joke (he was previously a comedy actor) by the West, his political opponents at home and by his enemies; there were few who didn't fear the worst when the invasion began.

However, Zelensky understood that modern warfare is fought in many dimensions, only one of which is the battlefield. His superpower is that he is a brave and effective communicator. His words, no less than those of Churchill in 1940, inspired his nation to fight back and galvanised the world to aid Ukraine in its plight, the clarity of his message thrown into relief by his opponent's leaden lies.

'I don't need a ride, I need ammunition,' he replied to Joe Biden's entreaties to escape. It is difficult to imagine a more perfect encapsulation of personal bravery, defiance, clarity and packaging.

Effective communication works.

When tackling any challenge, you must be clear-eyed and clear-headed about your baseline. However, you are not the only person who needs to understand the current situation. To succeed you must get buy-in from all your most important stakeholders, and ensure you keep them engaged throughout. This could be your team, bosses, board, colleagues, customers, clients or investors. Like much else, obvious but often not done well. Or even at all. This is why communication matters.

Jocko Willink, a former US Navy SEAL and now podcaster extraordinaire, tells how, after joining the SEAL Teams as a testosterone-fuelled youth, he realised that to progress he needed to learn to communicate effectively. In order to do so, he did a degree in English Literature and studied Shakespeare, amongst others. Learning to comprehend enabled him to learn to write well. Learning to write well, for him, became the basis for organised and clear thinking. Communication is about a lot more than being able to write snappy emails.

Use your baseline to get stakeholder alignment

Your initial objective is to ensure all stakeholders are aware of the reasoning that underpins your change programme (your baseline) and, most importantly, begin to build understanding of what is required of them and a case for what is in it for them. This is important because for some, if not all, it will entail an extended period of upheaval.

Your message should not simply be 'We need to change because . . .' Instead, over time, it must include why change is necessary, why that change is in the interests of the various groups who will need to endorse and support it, and what is likely to be required of them. Change is a team sport and you need as many people as possible on your side – a point we will return to in more detail in Chapter 5.

This communication is critical, and therefore requires a degree of care and attention. It is not a great idea to email all your customers and tell them you've decided your product is subpar and therefore you're going to change it. This may sound a ridiculous example, but my own industry, marketing services, has a long, inglorious (and, I hasten to add, unintended) history of taking exactly this approach.

How not to do it

Several years ago, one particularly venerable advertising agency set about a much discussed (in the bar of the Groucho Club, at least) change programme. The agency's clients (at the time) filled the nation's cupboards, fridges, driveways and front rooms. Many had been clients for decades. However, times had changed, and the leadership correctly recognised that they needed to reset their reputation and product. They needed to change. To this end they hired a (very) big-shot new global leader.

So far, so good.

He then set about doing what new leaders the world over love to do: telling anyone who would listen that everything that preceded him was rubbish – that the problem was that everything was shit, and that he was the solution.

The consequence of this approach was that the company's large and long-standing clients interpreted this as the new CEO turning his back on the campaigns they had invested hundreds of millions of dollars in. Campaigns that they loved. They felt that not only did he have no respect for what his own business had being doing for years, but by extension, he also had none for theirs.

This business no longer exists, and it is far from an isolated example.

This is a classic and, if extreme, familiar example of (very) poor stakeholder management. It is not enough to simply identify the nature of the problem and the need to change. As we've discussed, this is nearly always quite easy. In this example, everyone familiar with the business would have agreed that change was needed – even their clients, who were faced with similar challenges. The new CEO's fatal mistake was his failure to explain to some of his most important stakeholders why and how his change programme was in their interest. Instead, from his statements they concluded that he considered them to be the problem. Which, in truth, is exactly what I believe he really thought.

Identify your stakeholders and treat them extremely well

Effective stakeholder management is critical to your success. You must identify who yours are and ensure you communicate effectively with them. For anyone leading change their most important stakeholders are often the most neglected: the people in the team(s) that work for them. The vast majority will also have at least two others.

- **Boss(es) – those above you in the hierarchy**
This group are rarely neglected, but often poorly managed. Make sure you have an honest and transparent relationship with them.

- **Customers and clients**
Companies spend a lot of time communicating with their customers, but they often don't treat them as stakeholders. Make sure you bring them along with you. By asking their opinions, seeking their feedback and being clear why change is in their interests you avoid the pitfalls described above. Do this well and you may even turn them into your greatest advocates.

You must ensure your primary stakeholders are familiar with not just the nature of the challenges to be faced, but why it is in their interests to partner with you on the journey. Change is never a one-off event; rather it is a continuous and often lengthy process. An informed, intelligent and ongoing dialogue with all stakeholders is a powerful and effective way to build a coalition who are invested emotionally and physically, and who will remain firmly on your side throughout.

A simple guide for effective business communication

Effective communication is a large and important topic, one that goes beyond the scope of this book. However, the ability to do it well, or conversely the failure to do so, will have a significant bearing on your success. Throughout, you will need to ensure your teams and stakeholders are aligned, everybody is clear on their roles and objectives; obstacles must be overcome and lessons learnt. At every stage, effective and frequent communication will be required of you and those around you. It is a topic you should take care to do well. The following eight-point checklist* will ensure you stay on track.

1. State your objectives

Don't make the audience guess what the purpose of your communication is. Ask yourself:

- Why am I communicating?
- What do I want to achieve?
- Who am I primarily talking to?
- What do I want them most to remember?
- What do I want them to do as a result?

Remember my old boss's advice: sometimes pre-digested is the way to go.

---

* For more on the power of checklists, see my previous book, *No Bullsh*t Leadership.*

2. Be focused

A common problem with all communication (and especially business communication) is the desire to say too much. It's understandable – you have much you'd like to say. However, if you want your message to cut through and stick, you must focus on the most important aspects; **make it as long as it needs to be, and no longer**.

A good rule of thumb when standing before an audience is that, even for the most well-written and interesting presentation, **they will remember no more than three things**. You need to ensure these are the three things that matter to you. You can be wordy and self-indulgent when you're crafting your novel, but not when writing all-staff emails.

3. Identify your red thread

In Greek myth, Theseus escaped the Minotaur's labyrinth by following a red thread that he unravelled from his cloak as he went.

To avoid making your communications as confusing as a Cretan labyrinth, keep to a consistent theme. This is one reason why the KPIs of your baseline are so important – they can become your red thread. **Through continual reinforcement you will rapidly build awareness and comprehension of the task in hand.**

Identify your red thread, ensure you have enough content to achieve your objective and cut everything else.

4. Be clear

This is a prerequisite for all effective communication, yet one that is very often abandoned, particularly in the parallel universe of business-bullshit.

In his book *To Be Clear*, Philip Collins, former speech writer for Tony Blair, bemoans the poor quality of much business communication. The best thing you can do, he argues in his introduction, 'is to be as simple, as precise and as brief as you can, consistent with saying all of what you mean and not a word more, or indeed less'.

Collins concludes, '[Business executives] need to stop talking in code and **have the courage to be plain, in the knowledge that they have something to say and it would be better for the world to understand what it was**.'

Enough said.

5. Put your audience first

Communication is not about you (irrespective of how nervous you may feel as you step up to the stage). It's about your audience. You want them to think, understand or feel something, which is why you're there. And, even more importantly, you want them to remember it and you. **Make sure you are writing for them, not yourself.**

If you lead large teams, then, for many, your public communication may be the most regular – and per-haps the only – connection they have with you. If you've done your homework well you will readily be able to describe the nature of your baseline and, in time, your objectives and the stages along the way. However, at every step you must consider not just the functional and rational but the human and emotional. All change ultimately comes down to changing the behaviours of people; therefore you must be able to connect with your teams in language and terms that matter to them. This isn't as difficult as it might sound if you just spend a little time thinking about your communication from their perspective. This is another reason why your data collection, focus groups and bubble-bursting matter so much: the better you know your audience, the better you can communicate with them. A little empathy goes a long way.

6. Tell a story

We all understand stories. At their most basic, they need a start, middle and end. You must be able to describe the light as well as the shade, the sunlit uplands as well as the struggles that may lie ahead. Here, balance matters. You cannot simply trowel on all the bad news; you need to create a narrative that links problem to solution even if, at points of your change journey, the solution might appear somewhat threadbare.

Good communicators are good story tellers, and good stories aid comprehension, relevance and recall.

7. Communicate frequently and consistently

Say a relatively small number of things, be clear, consistent and say them often. It's the easiest (as well as the most under-appreciated and frequently forgotten) aspect of business communication – not least when it comes to the implementation of change programmes.

You are only a small part of people's lives (sorry to break it to you). They receive thousands of messages every day, from Instagram ads to angry emails from clients. You have to make sure you cut through this, and doing so requires consistency and frequency.

Don't overcomplicate, but do over-communicate.

8. Get help if you need it

This is probably the most important piece of advice I can offer, and one I also believe will be the most widely ignored. Communicating effectively is a skill; like any other skill it can be learnt, and with practice it can be improved. (We cover learning in more detail in Chapter 8.)

Communication comes in many forms: written and spoken, presentations and speeches, meetings formal and informal, media interviews and so on. All have their place. You must first ask yourself which are most important to your success right now and also how good you are at them. If you're not sure – ask somebody. For example, if you rarely need to do media interviews, don't waste time getting media trained. In my experience, senior executives love getting media trained but they rarely use it, and they rarely get presentation training even though very many would benefit from it. If you lack confidence speaking in front of large groups yet need to do it often, then get coaching in how to do it. It's obvious, but so many just blunder their way through. Don't.

It really is that important. If there are parts of communication that you aren't good enough at, then get help. We routinely do this in other areas. Some people are excellent writers, for example; if you're not, ask for help or find someone who is. It will be time and money well spent.

NO BULLSH*T COMMUNICATION

Communication is critical to success. In order to succeed,
effective and frequent communication is required by you
and of those around you at every stage.
Take care to do it well.

State your objectives

Don't make your audience guess the purpose and role of your
communication.

Be focused

Make it as long as it needs to be, and no longer.

Identify your red thread

Typically this is comprised of the themes defined by your baseline.

Be clear

Avoid jargon, buzzwords, verbosity and fluff.

Put your audience first

The better you understand your audience, the better you can communicate with them. A little empathy goes a long way.

Tell a story

It will aid comprehension, relevance and recall.

Communicate frequently and consistently

Don't overcomplicate, but do over-communicate.

Get help if you need it

Seek help and training in the skills you lack but need.

3

OBJECTIVE

To lead a successful change programme you must have a clear, ambitious objective, one that is motivating, persuasive and easily understood. This will provide a focal point around which your strategy, culture and team align.

There are times when a leader must move out ahead of the flock, go off in a new direction, confident that he is leading his people the right way.
Nelson Mandela

Make your vision so clear, your fears become irrelevant.
Anonymous

WHERE THE BASELINE IS ROOTED in observation, data and fact, the objective should be lofty and ambitious, delineating an outcome that is possibly quite distant at first, and that may evolve over time. It is not necessarily a response to the baseline, but the baseline is indispensable in determining how your journey toward it will begin.

Critical and self-evident though this task is, there is more bullshit taught on the subject than perhaps any other in the mountain of literature on change. This bullshit not only inhibits clear thinking and decision making; at its worst, it can derail change programmes before they've even begun. In defining their objective, leaders are encouraged to believe that they must strive not just for direction, but for elegance, poetry and even (and many well-known programmes insist on this) unique-ness. This chimeric search for a clever, pithy and elegant definition makes it harder for leaders to settle on a useful set of words to describe their objective and obscures its full utility and purpose.

A no bullsh*t objective

An objective is the leader's north star. The baseline is so important because it describes context, typically a mix of internal and external factors. The objective is where your change programme will take you.

It's impossible to generalise a solution, but it *is* possible to describe a few clear and simple rules:

- Don't overcomplicate.
- Be bold and ambitious.
- Favour clarity over brevity.
- Aim for a territory rather than the head of a pin.

Useful and clear examples include:

- Be the biggest.
- Have the best customer service.
- Be the most innovative.
- Have the largest market share.
- Have the best Ofsted score* in the county.
- Win the league.

---

* A UK-based system of measuring school performance.

- Transition from a leading valve manufacturer to a leading microchip manufacturer.
- Achieve a valuation of $100 million at sale.
- Start getting vaccines into arms in under twelve months.

All of these are incredibly easy to say (this list took me about two minutes to write), and for the vast majority of teams and organisations they would be a significant improvement on where they are today. However, because all are as difficult to do as they are easy to write, they would also be dismissed by as many as being unrealistic. Hence the pressing need for more leaders capable of leading change.

The last on the list is one you will be familiar with. Here the baseline was (as is often the case) easy. The world faced a generational threat from a new and deadly disease. There was lots of data, but it was all saying pretty much the same thing: that the creation, manufacture, testing and distribution of vaccines is, as we all now know, fiendishly complicated.

The UK government made, with exemplary speed, three good decisions:

1. They recognised that their usual processes and systems were completely unsuited for such an objective. They had to change.
2. They needed the right leader in charge, someone with both category expertise and proven leadership experience. Crucially, they also quickly recognised

that they did not have that person in their current
structure and would have to look outside.
3. They would give that person the necessary authority
to make decisions and get things done; the achievement of the objective would justify the means.

Their appointment of Kate Bingham wasn't without
controversy. However, in our no bullshit world, we're
interested only in results, and Bingham's programme to
select, procure and manufacture vaccines was a classic
example of what can be achieved when baseline, objective,
leadership ability and culture align.

The uniqueness trap

So much energy and money has been thrown into the
search for 'perfect' objectives that many leaders come to
see this as a quest not for direction but wit and wisdom,
to the extent that this search can become an end in itself
– a demonstration of intelligence and leadership virility.
As a consequence, I have seen teams (and indeed been
part of teams) that have spent so long agonising over this
decision that they have failed to ever truly move beyond
it. This I urge you to avoid at all costs; it, by definition,
guarantees failure.

A common pitfall is the search for uniqueness. Not
only is this unnecessary, it is nearly always impossible.
The vast majority of organisations are simply seeking
to do a common thing better than the competition. This
is certainly the case in a business or sporting context,

and by analogy it also applies to an array of other areas, such as education or research. In none of these is there a requirement to be unique, and it is never a prerequisite for success. The search for uniqueness when trying to clearly define an objective is a time consuming (and energy-sapping) distraction from the task in hand. Yet it is a common reason that so many change programmes fail before they have even begun.

Trigger warning

The level of hyperbole and nonsense the Leadership Industrial Complex can reach in 'helping' leaders find their 'objective' knows no limit. I was once invited to attend a two-day residential course to define the 'purpose' for a well-known household brand. It was run by outside consultants using their 'proprietary' methodology. This, it was explained, relied on using the methods and spiritualism of Native Americans (in case you were wondering, they were all British, and it was held in a residential hotel in Surrey, a rather posh county conveniently close to London). I've managed to blot most of the experience from my memory, but I do clearly remember one task. We were sent off individually to walk the grounds and collect items from nature – flowers, pebbles, feathers and the like – from which we would, through some mystical process, gain inspiration, allowing us to define the brand's purpose. On our return we placed our chosen item reverentially in the middle of the circle of attendees and … oh God. Anyway, it's too horrible to have to relive it.

In that example I was simply an attendee, but before I become too smug and all-knowing, I must first remove the plank from my own eye. I too have sat in many off-sites and spent hours, sometimes with just the team, sometimes with outside consultants, desperately searching for clever and unique words to describe what it is we wished to become. I thought it was what leaders were supposed to do. Spoiler alert: it isn't.

So defining has this task become, in the minds of many – that of identifying the objective (or whatever word you wish to use: ambition, vision, purpose, etc.) – that it is the first thing they leap into when presented with a new role or challenge. Not in itself a bad thing, assuming they also pay attention to their baseline as well, of course. The problem is, because we are told that it has to be clever, snappy and unique, many never get beyond trying to answer this question at all. Round and round they go, trying to find that illusive set of words that, once found, will unlock everything.

It's a classic opportunity for group-think. At the end of a long two days, and desperate for the weekend, the group finally agrees on a set of words. Freed, everyone heads home, glad to have agreed on something, anything, and relieved to escape. However, when Monday comes they discover to their dismay that they all have a different recollection of what it was that had been decided. And worse, when shared with someone who hadn't been in the room, the response is underwhelmed blank stares. We've all been there. Maybe you're reading this because you're stuck there right now.

Take a common task and do it uncommonly well

Every task is different, and in some (perhaps many) cases it may be possible and/or necessary for your objective to be very specific. For example, the task in hand may, by its very nature, require a clearly defined set of parameters. In this case, defining the end point is easier than usual: simply spell them out. For example, a sports team may wish to win the league. Or an engineering team may have to remedy a specific fault in a new R&D project. That's it. Done. That wasn't so hard. What *is* hard, as always, is getting on and doing it.

Alternatively, and more commonly, your goal may be both broad and distant, in time and in ambition. Here it may be difficult and even undesirable to attempt to be too specific too early. A team may decide, as I once did in a company I ran, that the primary task is to create a culture capable of outperforming its competitors. In our case, we had an initial go at defining the culture we wanted, but this inevitably evolved over time – as you would expect. But at the start it was enough to know two things. The first was that the focus of our strategy was in the implementation of the culture we believed would enable us to succeed, and the second was that we would give our culture a name, 'Open'.

We knew that its defining characteristic would be the opposite of a top-down hierarchy – the situation that we found ourselves in at the beginning and that we had determined to rip apart. Having very clearly defined our start point, broadly outlined our objective and spent a lot of time communicating and seeking buy-in from the company, we initially moved with great urgency and focus. Then, over the following years, we refined and adjusted our objective – not discarding it, but sharpening how we described it, while keeping our, and everybody else's, eyes firmly fixed on the unifying concept of 'Open'.

There was nothing at all unique about the idea (at the time of writing, if you google 'open culture' you get 4.15 billion results), nor about the behaviour or language we gradually built around this ambition. However, we were convinced that if we did this well we would thrive, and that indeed proved to be the case. Before long, we and others were writing case studies about our version of 'open culture', and even the World Cup-winning rugby coach Sir Clive Woodward was impressed, saying, 'I love working with [this business]. Anybody who has an interest in a team's culture and its impact should spend a couple of hours listening to their story.'

I'm sure many will quibble about what is objective and strategy, or even that to have a culture as an objective made no sense. Feel free. But there's no right and wrong, only what works and what doesn't. Although nothing we did was original or unique, we took a common thing and did it unusually well – which in nearly all circumstances will put you very close to the top of the pile.

Migration

Sometimes it is useful to imagine change as analogous to a railway journey, one that follows a set path between two clear and tightly defined points. However, in large, complicated organisations or situations, this can impose a rigidity of thought and deed that may ultimately be unhelpful. Certainly you don't have to be as precise in your language as this approach implies.

A CEO of a large retailer, who at the time was in the foothills of their change programme, described their plan to me as a migration. She imagined the organisation as a huge flock of birds, loosely but clearly bound together by their common direction. They knew exactly where they were at the beginning (of course), and were clear on their direction, but were initially very broad in defining their destination. Her level of specificity declined the further into the future she looked. I imagine it as looking down a cone, holding the narrow end near your eye.

This is a very practical, action-focused and therefore useful thought experiment. It encourages immediate action, has a built-in acceptance of course corrections *en route*, and allows the destination to be sharpened and brought into increasingly clear focus as the journey progresses. Most of all, it has the (perhaps unusual) merit of honesty. It is how change works in practice, whether business schools like it or not.

The four critical roles an objective should play

The objective is most easily understood as the end point of your change journey. This is self-evident. Various words are used here, among them ambition, vision and purpose, but they all aim to do the same thing. Don't get hung up on language, just use the words and description that work best for you, and which can be clearly and easily understood by everyone involved. Brevity is good, but clarity is more important. Clarity aids comprehension and recollection. A clear and well-written objective should provide a signpost for decision-making and an ongoing guide for action. And remember, you can always sharpen your thinking over time.

In leading change there are four important roles that your objective should play:

1. Set destination and direction
This is obvious, and needs little explanation. It should be a simple and clearly understood description of what it is you are attempting to achieve, allowing you to set milestones and to course-correct along the way.

2. Aid decision-making
A clear, universally understood objective provides a framework for the critical decisions that must be taken for your programme to succeed.

3. Build coalitions
Whatever the size of your organisation or challenge, there are multiple stakeholders you need to communicate with regularly. A simple, clear objective is critical to building the coalition you need for success.

4. Enable alignment
This is one of the most important, and yet possibly

the most commonly overlooked, advantages of a clear objective. Your immediate team are your most important allies, and a clear objective allows you to keep that team tightly aligned and effective. Crucially, it provides a framework for the difficult and challenging conversations that all teams need to have in order to keep them fit and healthy.

Dealing politely with double faults

In tennis, doubles is a rather different game to singles, as anyone who has played knows. In singles, as the name suggests, you face your opponent alone (along with your inner voice, of course, all too often reproachful, judgemental or even angry). In doubles, however, you are part of a team, and the most effective teams find a way to outperform.

I recently joined a tennis team that plays in a league and comprises four people playing in two pairs. It started as a bit of a lark (I hadn't played team tennis for a decade), and it was just a relief to be out of the house after endless lockdowns. However, we started to do quite well, and suddenly it began to matter whether we won or not.

Tennis is a difficult game. One of the problems with doubles is that your internal voice, what Dr Steve Peters in his book *The Chimp Paradox* refers to as our 'Inner Chimp', now starts chattering away, not just about your own game, but that of your partner also. There are few things more annoying than when, at 30–30, after you hit a great first serve, your partner dumps a gimme volley into the net. Odds are you're so pissed off (chimp chattering away) that you hit a double fault next, and that's your serve gone. 'And none of it was your fault, was it?' the chimp gleefully points out, before stuffing another banana in his mouth.

My partner and I decided we needed to take it all a bit more seriously. We bought those awful energy gels beloved of cyclists, and he ordered extra packets of Fisherman's Friends (for the uninitiated, they are a very strong and somewhat odd-flavoured lozenge – he claimed they helped him concentrate). Most importantly we began to talk to each other. Not only during the game, but before it.

Before every match we would discuss what we were each going to try to do. This was simple stuff: serve-volley (or not), return cross court (rather than glory shots down the line), be patient, be aggressive and so on. These, as you will have noted, were not complicated match strategies. However, what was revolutionary (for us at least) was that, in openly sharing our objectives (with the implicit collective aim of winning the match), we each gave the other permission to talk about our game, during the game. The purpose of the pre-match discussion was therefore directed not at our opponents but at ourselves. There is no hierarchy in a doubles team – no boss, leader or follower, simply peers, even if they barely know each other. Our pre-match alignment allowed us to have quite difficult conversations at points of tension and pressure – with ease.

The power of alignment

An aligned team doesn't just know where it's trying to get to; it uses that common objective to outline individual

roles and define interpersonal relationships. This alignment provides the team's members with a framework for
powerful and otherwise difficult conversations.

Imagine this as depersonalising the personal. The
reason some conversations are difficult, and therefore
often avoided, is because we perceive them to be personal.
And in a team, they often are. Yet an effective team needs
to be able to have difficult conversations without falling
out. It's easy to say but difficult to do, especially if the
context is pressured and stressful. However, clear buy-in
and alignment to the shared objective allows difficult
conversations to be had in the context of the objective,
rather than appearing to be an unwanted, perhaps even
unwarranted, personal critique. Without alignment, these
conversations quite often either are not had at all, become
rows or simmering resentments, and of course can lead
to the toxicity of office politics. Just because things aren't
being said doesn't mean they aren't being thought.

Back on the court, we were aligned; we weren't two
individuals, we were a team. It became OK to ask why
the other had hit a particular shot, or indeed to tell them
to stop doing it if it went against what they had said they
were going to try to do. It allowed us to discuss honestly
how we were each playing and feeling (in tennis these
two are essentially one and the same), to coach each other,
to change our minds and to problem-solve as the match
progressed. It allowed us to have effective conversations
about how we were going to achieve our objective.

The primary role the pre-match conversation played
was not to clarify the overall task (that was glaringly

obvious); rather, in sharing personal objectives, we created alignment between us. And alignment affords teams that invaluable tool: effective communication. Alignment allowed us to talk to each other about things that had previously not just been unspoken, but caused us to seethe and negatively affected our own game. Although here I have to admit, it is still infuriating if your partner dumps a simple volley into the net on your serve – the only worse feeling being if it is you who has missed the volley.

In my experience, leaders and leadership teams, even those who have successfully agreed on their objective, often fail to use that clarity to align themselves with one another. A clear objective gives you the opportunity to build effective relationships within your leadership group, which in turn form the basis for an effective organisational culture.

A four-point programme to align your team

1. Have a clear objective

Ensure you have a common and clearly understood objective.

2. Ask what's in it for them

Discuss with the team what their personal ambitions are and work to ensure that you have a mutual understanding of what it is about the shared vision that motivates them personally.

3. **Anticipate conflict**

Conflict and disagreement are an essential part of an effective, functioning team. Discuss how you want to deal with conflictual situations before they arise. How will you hold each other to account?

4. **Keep doing it**

Practice makes perfect. Get used to reviewing your progress. Giselle Mather, Director of Rugby at Wasps (a Premiership rugby club) and a World Cup winner, talks of how, after every match, her team has a full and frank debrief. They are, she says, incredibly powerful, but only really work if everyone is able to be completely honest. The more often you have honest and respectful conversations, the easier and less conflictual they become.

The five rules for powerful and effective objectives

The objective of this book is to liberate you from orthodoxy and the drudgery of conventional change theory, to inspire you to think differently about how to define effective objectives, and how to use them well. What follows are five simple and universal rules to help you find an objective that does what you need it to do and hopefully reduces the chances of you finding yourself wandering around a field in Surrey wondering if taking back a lump of cow shit on a stick as your source of inspiration will get you fired by the client.

1. Be (very) ambitious

An objective must be imbued with genuine, perhaps unreasonable, ambition. Here at least, the Leadership Industrial Complex and I almost agree.

Your objective should be for your organisation to be the best, the fastest, the most innovative; to reverse a precipitous decline; to achieve results never before thought possible; to change entrenched behaviours or beliefs; to lift people's eyes from the day-to-day to believe that things can be different, and that they themselves will be part of making that happen.

It's scary, of course, but also invigorating, even thrilling. Who wouldn't want to be responsible for that? The more explicit you are about the scale of your ambition, the more you can be seen to fail. That's why leadership – great leadership – is hard. But that's why you're here, right? You don't want to be a manager, you want to create an earthquake, a revolution. And that requires a big, scary statement of ambition right at the start.

2. Be inspiring and sincere

It is of fundamental importance to all change programmes that everyone (or as many as are realistically possible) feels engaged and inspired by the task at hand. To achieve anything worthwhile requires a combination of culture and ambition that inspire your teams to outperform. Easy to say, difficult to do.

Inspiration in a leadership context is a rather

difficult concept to wrap our arms around. This is one of the reasons that leaders tie themselves in knots trying to navigate their desire to make their business better, while promising their employees magnificent high-order reasons to come to work – promises they often struggle to keep. An obviously self-defeating outcome. The best advice I can give is to be honest and sincere, and to not overthink it. It is perfectly possible for your teams to feel inspired without being told they are also saving the world.

A more realistic, effective and, indeed, honest approach is to aspire to be an organisation that achieves success in its own right, while also taking a responsible and engaged approach to wider society, to the local community and to its employees. Such an objective, done with sincerity, will represent a very serious and responsible stretch target. if everyone actually did this (rather than talking vaguely about it), the collective societal transformation would be enormous. And it goes without saying that, for many employees, this would be a dramatic improvement on their current experience.

So be ambitious, honest and sincere. If you manage that, then you're well ahead of the pack.

3. Choose clarity over brevity

If in doubt, opt for clarity over brevity. So much of what we are told encourages leaders to do the opposite. If you need to take a couple of sentences to get it right, don't worry about it. As you live with it and begin to make progress you'll be surprised how quickly you sharpen your thinking and therefore wording. And as people become more familiar with it, you can shorthand, as we did with Open. Indeed, counter-intuitively, we discovered that the more we tried to explain Open, the more complicated and less comprehensible it seemed to become.

Clarity allows for more than just comprehension. It enables recollection and, crucially, accelerates the process by which members of the wider team are able to understand their individual roles in the change programme.

Whatever you decide, it is critical that all stakeholders can understand it, remember it and, ideally, see how achieving it will be of benefit to them.

4. Over-communicate

We covered communication in the previous chapter, but it is critical in bringing your vision to life.

Too many leaders spend way too long deciding what it is they want to do, and then way too little time and effort explaining their thinking to their stakeholders. Consistent, clear and regular communication is possibly the single easiest action leaders at all levels could take that would dramatically improve their likelihood of success.

This is why clarity and simplicity matter so much. It is so much easier to communicate your objective if it is easy to explain and remember. But even so, you will need to communicate at every opportunity and far more frequently than you think. This can sometimes be shorthand, sometimes in greater detail, but far better that people get bored of the repeated message than forget it or aren't aware of it. And to be clear, you'll get bored long before everyone else does, so keep going.

I once wrote our company's objectives in three words on a simple piece of polyboard, and at every company meeting, no matter the topic, at some point I would hold it up and link what we were discussing back to our three words. It was deliberately low-tech, and over time the board became dog-eared and worn, my waving it around being a source of amusement and ribbing. But it worked. The more people joked about it, the more the three words became part of our language and lore. I meet people fifteen years and two jobs later who ask if I still have it. (Of course I don't. It was only a bit of polyboard.)

So don't overthink, but do over-communicate.

5. Foster collective ownership
The objective can't simply belong to you, even if in reality this is initially the case. For you to be successful you have to take it on a journey from comprehension, through relevance, to collective ownership. In fact, it has often struck me that one measure of a successful change programme is the ownership journey of the objective itself. If it can morph from the possession of one (you or, more commonly, a small group) to the possession of all, and if, as I do, you consider change

to be primarily about changing individual behaviours, then you really are well on your way.

The big challenge, as ever, is how. In small teams it should be relatively easy, but in larger organisations this can require significant effort and time. But this will be time well spent.

The first step is awareness. The second is comprehension and, more specifically, comprehension of what it means for each individual, shifting the objective from a corporate aspiration to a source of individual action.

This can be difficult. You need to be realistic; people are not sitting expectantly waiting to catch your distant-uttered pearls of wisdom. You need a programme of awareness, comprehension and buy-in. This is often mis-characterised as helping everybody understand what you think. Instead, through smart consultation, communication and discussion, you should aim to make everyone feel like they own a share in the objective.

Don't be afraid of discussion or even disagreement – indeed you should encourage and enable both. It is better for people to have a chance to voice their opinions than to keep them hidden away or moaned about in secret. Furthermore, discussion enables comprehension and engagement encourages shared ownership, both of which are hugely beneficial to your chances of success. This doesn't require you to agree with all that is said, but it does give you an opportunity to explain your thinking and help people understand what's in it for them. And, of course, sometimes you will agree; great ideas will emerge if you allow them the time and space to do so. Here again, beware the effects of hierarchy. And to be asked questions at all demonstrates a relatively high degree of engagement and understanding.

In all but the smallest teams it is impossible for you to directly engage with the majority of people in this process. Nor is the point for there to be decision by committee – anything but. Rather you should find ways to enable people to independently discuss, share and build on your leadership team's thinking. We have already covered (in Chapter 1) some straightforward ways to do this, and I would encourage you to explore some of these (such as small focus groups) at this stage. These can be used to explain your thinking, get feedback and listen to ideas and suggestions, many of which will be very helpful and would otherwise remain unsaid, or be kept hidden from you.

Your objective in achieving widespread buy-in is not only to ensure everybody understands the collective direction, but also to enable everyone to understand what their individual role will be. Collective ownership gets you more than followers, it builds advocates and evangelists for your revolution.

A means to an end

Leaders are people. Leaders are you and me. It's easy for me to claim that objective-setting is straightforward, but in reality, perhaps it isn't. I can imagine some wanting to believe, but reflecting on the challenges they face right now, and it not feeling anything like so straightforward.

I'm not trivialising the challenge, I'm simply arguing that setting an effective objective, one that allows you to begin, that can galvanise your team and get you all going in the same direction, need not be as daunting as we are led to believe.

The more we build it up, the more setting an objective becomes an end in itself. Many leaders make this process so complicated that they never get beyond it. Finding an objective that is ambitious and succinct, one that everybody agrees to, one that is useful and unique, is all but impossible; it is certainly very time consuming and difficult. Therefore it often doesn't get done at all. And, if it doesn't get done, how do you know where you're going, never mind describe your journey to anybody else. It is a common, yet often unseen cause of failure.

If you find yourself in this place, don't beat yourself up. You're far from alone. I've been there many times. Take the pressure off. Make the problem more manageable by making it smaller. Think of it as the creation not of a set of stone tablets but of sheets of paper; rather than a beautifully crafted aphorism, a paragraph of simple prose; rather than a postage stamp, a ballpark.

Write first in pencil

For an action-focused leader, as you must be, it is better to write your objective in pencil, quickly, and set about executing against it, than to tread with leaden feet towards a corporate-speak set of stone-carved words, examples of which we are all familiar.

Defining a clear objective is a critical aspect of any leader's task, and (as with understanding the nature of your challenge) while it certainly requires effort, boldness and imagination, it isn't a difficult task. Change requires great urgency and energy (as we shall see), and it is better to get quickly to an objective that over time you refine and improve than to slog slowly toward an unlikely version of perfection – while your competitors, or technology, or your employees slowly leave you behind. So write first in pencil and be prepared to improve (and learn) as you go.

Your objective is not disposable, but nor is it unchangeable. It is a tool, and you should see it as such. It isn't the end, it is simply a means to describe your journey. Make the task of defining your objective (if not its ambition) feel smaller, less permanent and you'll find yourself liberated to begin. Because something impermanent can change and evolve, which in reality is exactly what you want.

NO BULLSH*T OBJECTIVE

To lead a successful change programme you must have a clear,
ambitious objective, one that is motivating, persuasive and
easily understood. This will provide a focal point around
which your strategy, culture and team align.

Take a common task and do it uncommonly well

Don't overcomplicate.
Be bold and ambitious.
Favour clarity over brevity.
Aim for a territory rather than the head of a pin.

The four critical roles an objective should play

1. Set destination and direction.
2. Aid decision-making.
3. Build coalitions.
4. Achieve team alignment.

Achieving alignment within your team

Ensure you have a common and clearly understood objective.
Understand what it is about the shared objective that motivates
them personally.
Discuss how to deal with conflictual situations before they arise.
The more often you have honest conversations, the easier and less
conflictual they become.

Five rules for powerful and effective objectives

1. Show genuine, perhaps unreasonable, ambition.
2. Be inspiring, honest and sincere.
3. Choose clarity over brevity.
4. Over-communicate.
5. Foster collective ownership.

Write first in pencil

Your objective is not disposable, but nor should it be unchangeable.
It is simply a means to describe your journey.

4

BREAKING FREE

Change is a physical activity that does not begin until you act.
The leader's most immediate task is convincing their team that
change is not just desirable, but that it is going to happen. And fast.
That whatever else, tomorrow is going to be different to today,
that next week will be different to this week, that they are not
the latest in a long line doomed to fail.

Ere we are, Monday morning; day after tomorrow
Wednesday and nowt done yet.
Anonymous Yorkshire farmer (*c.* 1960), as quoted in
The Times

I'm not interested in your stories about the past or any
crap of that kind because the woods are burning, boys,
you understand?
Arthur Miller, *Death of a Salesman*

THERE'S A SCENE IN ARMANDO IANNUCCI'S superb satire of
Westminster party politics, *The Thick of It*, where the min-
ister of state, Hugh Abbot, is threatened yet again with
being fired by Peter Capaldi's terrifying super-sweary
spin doctor, Malcolm Tucker.

While Hugh frets, sweats and grovels, his PR director,
Terri, gossips maliciously on her desk phone in the office
outside. We watch her as though glimpsed through a
half-open door: 'It's probably going to be Hugh that has to
go this time,' she whispers *sotto voce*, before rocking back
and belly laughing at the unheard reply. 'Oh it'll be fine
in the end. We'll just get another middle-aged man in on

Monday morning; come through the door, stride around a bit, spunk off and I'll have to clear up the mess. It'll be business as usual,' she concludes reassuringly. A *cri de cœur* for civil servants everywhere.

The Thick of It, a hardly veiled commentary on the Blair years, aside from being one of the most sharply observed and best-written shows of the early noughties, is a study in cynical incompetence. A government department elected to drive change focuses on nothing but their own paranoia. Policy is simply a means to their personal end. There is no objective, strategy or action that goes beyond the preservation of their position for twenty-four more hours. With hindsight, it seems a more innocent time.

For a leader it is the anti-manual, the wax that vanishes from the mould. However, we would be wise not to laugh (or judge) without a little self-reflection. Who among us hasn't been Terri, gossiping and damning the new and incoming tribe, the next in a long line of noisy, opinionated and ultimately doomed leaders.

I have many times stood before an audience, their arms folded, and described the need to change – why I was there, the challenges the business faced and my new ambitions. Hundreds of pairs of eyes look back at me as though they'd heard it all before. And I'm sure they had. For some I am an object of curiosity perhaps, maybe interest, maybe opportunity. Others fret and worry.

However, at such moments my greatest fear is to be dismissed by the audience as simply 'Hugh's successor', the latest in a long line doomed to fail; that my audience calculates (based on their past experience) that I'm just like all the others, that in fact they don't need to engage with me or my words at all. They can just hunker down, try to keep out of the way and, soon enough, I too will be gone. After the initial flurry of enthusiastic emails and perhaps a few glasses at a warm-sauvignon get-together, it will be, as Terri described, business as usual.

Your task as a leader of change is, above all else, to ensure it will be anything but.

The leadership equation

If you remember only two words as a change leader, make them 'clarity' and 'action'. In my previous book, *No Bullsh*t Leadership*, I described their relationship as the 'leadership equation'. It is a powerful tool for all leaders:

impact = clarity x action

In the equation, clarity is represented by all the topics we usually think of when we think about leadership (and change), for example: strategy, values, culture, research, focus groups, competitor analysis, market context, structure and so on.

However, the primary purpose of the equation is to encourage leader's bias toward action. Clarity, though critical, is not leadership. Without action, the sum total of change is zero, and failure is guaranteed:

impact = clarity x action
If action = 0, impact = 0.
Simple maths, but a powerful conclusion.

The 40/70 rule

The US general and politician Colin Powell perfectly captured the balance effective leaders must strike. In *No Bullsh*t Leadership*, I also introduced Powell's 40/70 rule:

> *Don't take action if you have only enough information to give you a less than 40 per cent chance of being right, but if you have waited until you're more than 70 per cent certain then you've waited too long.*

The 40/70 rule is a smart encapsulation of how to take action in the real world, one where contexts change, where external and internal forces pull to and fro. A decision is a choice taken when the outcome is uncertain, and the 40/70 rule encourages leaders to recognise this and act anyway. Because without action, failure is guaranteed.

Clarity

In the specific case of change programmes, Clarity can be understood as being the sum of two primary tasks that are the distillation of the outputs from Chapters 1, 2 and 3:

1. **Direction**: the imaginary line drawn from **baseline** to **objective**.

2. **Communication**: **ensuring that all your stakeholders are clear** on the need to change, the direction you are headed and why that is a good thing for them (in the extreme, perhaps the only way to avoid ruin).

The liberation of action

The point of the leadership equation is that change does not begin until you take action. Objectives and strategy are crucial – if you don't know where you're going then you're never going to get there. But if you don't take action then objectives and strategy are just fantasy.

If clarity is the sum of direction and communication, then:

impact = (direction + communication) x action

Wonderful and clever thinking is worthless without action. But even if your strategy is imperfect, as it inevitably will be, or your communication is inelegant, as it sometimes will be, a bias toward action will still deliver impact and change.

Many change programmes founder not for want of ideas and sincere intentions, but effective, consistent and long-term action. Much of which cannot be pre-baked, but is a consequence, as we will see in Chapter 8, of continual learning and reorientation. The absence of effective action, evaluation and reaction is the surest guarantee of failure.

Some change leaders fear action because they fear error; it's human and normal to do so. Missteps can be painful, and action, far more than writing PowerPoint decks, is where change programmes can be seen to stumble. However, leaders must recognise 'errors' as a necessary part of the process. An unexpected outcome does not mean failure, whereas inaction inevitably does.

Far from being a risk, action liberates. If a decision is a choice made when uncertain of the outcome, it is axiomatic that sometimes the outcome will not be as you hope or expect. Yet take them we must if we are to progress. As military staff colleges teach the world over, no plan survives contact with the enemy. For a change programme, the status quo is failure, and without effective action that is where you will remain.

Be less Hugh

As we established in Chapter 1, the greatest challenge in these moments is rarely that of explaining the nature of the task that lies before you. Nor is it difficult to explain the benefits of an improvement in that situation, even if for some this represents a worrying or uncertain prospect.

Change is a physical activity, and the leader's most immediate task is convincing their team that change is not just desirable, but that this time, it is going to happen. And fast. That whatever else, tomorrow is going to be different to today, that next week will be different to this week; that they are not, like the hapless Hugh Abbot, simply the latest in a long line doomed to fail.

Overcoming sticking friction

It's easier to move a sledge once you've freed it from the ice. Scientists refer to these two states as sticking friction and kinetic friction:

sticking friction > kinetic friction*

No matter the size, shape or weight of an object, the energy required to get it moving is *always* greater than the energy required to keep it in motion. Change works in the same way. As you begin, you may have to kick and struggle to get going, but once underway it becomes just that bit easier to keep moving.

Initially, direction matters less than movement

The first and most important action in leading a successful change programme is to break free. Breaking free means preparing the ground for the changes you must make to reach your objective. Here, somewhat counter-intuitively, direction matters less than movement. This is the opposite to what traditional change theory tells us.

Your first priority is to ensure that everyone believes that change, any change, is possible, that it is anything but business as usual. Words alone just won't cut it, no matter how inspiring and persuasive your speech.

This is freeing the sledge, and to do so you will have to push, pull, rock it from side to side, chip the ice from the runners, heave, shout and kick. Once free, altering direction is easier, it's getting the thing moving that's so damn difficult. So it is with change. Teams don't just appear out of thin air. Your arrival may be new, but belief, culture, trust, respect and confidence take time to develop. This is kinetic friction: these things will come in

---

* Sticking friction is always greater than kinetic friction.

time through your strategy and determined actions. To start, however, you need to focus on freeing the sledge and overcoming the resistance, cynicism, scepticism and inertia of the group.

At this stage some of the actions you take may not be directly related to your ultimate goal, but are simply designed to create an expectation, an understanding, that the status quo is no more; that you're not all talk, and change isn't simply coming, it's already here; that action and urgency are the order of the day.

Note: Just as with much else in this book, this approach can apply to individuals (you) as well as organisations.

Five powerful approaches to freeing the sledge

1. Environment

Environment is an underutilised and very powerful driver of change. Perhaps it's underutilised because it seems a little trivial, not Harvard Business School enough to count as a proper business strategy. But nobody who has been responsible for the redesign of an office seating plan and experienced the ensuing uproar would ever make such a mistake.

Freeing the sledge can best be understood as the breaking of (often very ingrained) habits. We couldn't get through life if we didn't do some things on autopilot, tasks our brains perform with a minimum of conscious effort. That's why, it is said, successful people wear the same style of clothes every day; it's just one less decision to take. To free the sledge, however, we must strive to push familiar tasks from the subconscious to the conscious. And a great way to do this is to use the environment.

Several years ago I was tasked with moving fifteen businesses in the same group into a single location. It was met with variable levels of enthusiasm by the leaders of the businesses concerned. I had been brought in halfway though the planning process and was assailed with strategy documents and lobbied relentlessly by CEOs determined to change as little as they possibly could. I threw them all out. The move was, as I saw it, an opportunity to reset the most fundamental principles of our culture, strategy and objectives. And I was determined to use the new location as a totem for that future.

It was an initially painful and difficult process, but within six months not only could everyone see and feel the almost immediate benefits, but the business's reputation and performance were on the way to a total transformation. The shouting, gnashing of teeth and threats of resignation were never mentioned again. Like all good ideas, it had become everybody's idea.

Where and how we work is a powerful cultural marker. There are very many quick, simple and effective ways to use geography and the environment to break habits and signal change. You can learn much about an organisation from its physical environment, everything from the decor and seating plan, to where people eat and meet. Does everyone have an office, just some people or no one? Where are the offices? Is the building quiet or noisy, full or empty, colourful or monochrome, messy or tidy, corporate or chaotic? The physical environment of an organisation tells you much about how it feels and thinks. Yet it is often overlooked, or seen as incidental to change programmes, put last on the list, rather than offering an early opportunity to break free. Put it first.

In recent years there has been much debate about open-plan working vs offices, fixed desks vs hot desks, home vs hybrid, etc., but these decisions are usually couched in terms of functional efficiency, rather than how they impact (for good or bad) the organisation's culture. An effective leader should use all the tools available to create the culture they need (and shake off those things they wish to leave behind). The environment is an overlooked and powerful lever.

It's an approach that works for teams and individuals, and in all environments. It's not about having a 'good' or 'bad' space, it's about physical change as a precursor to wider, more strategic changes that will come later. All teams develop (consciously or not) habits, shared behaviours and unwritten codes. Often these are so familiar that they are invisible even to ourselves. Your task is to break these by helping yourself and others see the familiar anew, making the unconscious, conscious. You'll be surprised how even small changes to the team environment can alter how it thinks, feels and acts.

In the opening passage of *Creativity, Inc.*, Ed Catmull, co-founder of Pixar, describes how seemingly insignificant details can mutate into enduring habits and negative behaviours. In their boardroom they had a large, beautiful table that had been designed and built specifically for the space. It was long, narrow and very expensive. For over a decade it was the hub around which they worked. All important meetings related to movie production were held in the room, meaning there were often more than thirty people squeezed along the table's sides.

The problem was, it made communication very difficult. If you were at either end you were effectively cut out of the discussion. Therefore, because it was critical that the producers, director, lead writers and other senior executives could contribute, they had to be placed in the centre. In time, to make this easier still, somebody had the idea of producing name cards to mark the 'important' people's places. As the company grew they incrementally and unintentionally found themselves with a caste system: those seated in the centre, those at the ends, and those unable to get places at the table at all, who sat round the edge of the room. A meeting designed to be about the free, open and unstructured flow of ideas had gradually and unwittingly introduced a hierarchy that actively inhibited discussion. The further you were from the centre the less important you appeared to be, and the more difficult and less likely it was for you to contribute.

Catmull observes: 'The seating arrangements and place cards were designed for the convenience of the leaders, including me. Sincerely believing that we were in an inclusive meeting, *we* saw nothing amiss because *we* didn't feel excluded. Those not sitting at the centre ... saw quite clearly it established a pecking order, but presumed we – the leaders – had intended that outcome.'

By chance, they happened one day to have the meeting in a smaller room with a square table and immediately saw what was wrong: 'The interplay was better, the exchange of ideas more free-flowing, the eye-contact automatic. Every person … felt free to speak up.'

Catmull demanded the dismantling of the expensive designer table. Place cards, now unnecessary, were discarded. He concludes: 'Unhindered communication was key [to Pixar's success], no matter your position. At our long skinny table, comfortable in our middle seats, we had utterly failed to recognize we were behaving contrary to that basic tenet.'

Be prepared here for cynicism and possibly even rebellion. But that's the point. An organisation's physical environment is something that affects everyone within it and has consequences, intended and unintended, for how people think, feel and behave. You want to use it to make people sit up and pay attention, to see that you're serious, to feel something new and different. This does not define your strategy, but it is a tangible new beginning.

People become very attached to where they sit, who they sit with, how they navigate the space and build their habits accordingly. Often, the more senior they are the more attached they become. But if you want to break free, here lies opportunity. By changing seating plans, department boundaries, meeting rooms and communal spaces, old habits and old customs can be shattered (I use that word deliberately) and renewal can begin. Change, at its core, is lots of individuals doing their thing differently. Your challenge is to find ways for your programme to cut through on an individual level. Initiating change to the physical environment is a powerful and effective way to achieve this. There will be opportunities everywhere if you are imaginative, clear-eyed and bold enough to hunt them out, whether in the home office or corporate HQ, classroom or lab.

2. Routines

Routines have their place, but they are also how we ingrain and sustain habits. Our objective here is to break habits, therefore we must break our routines.

The pandemic was the great breaker of routines. We had to let go of so much while simultaneously and rapidly learning new habits we would previously never have dreamed of: wearing masks, washing our hands for twenty seconds, not shaking hands, working from home, holding meetings by video, standing two metres apart – all became, and in some cases remain, the new normal.

The pandemic didn't just force us to break familiar routines; to our collective surprise, we discovered that many of them had not been necessary at all. I doubt if commuting and office life will ever return to exactly how they were, to pick two examples of many.

If habits as fundamental as these can change, how many more opportunities, big and small, surround you and your team right now? Some will be so ingrained that you will not initially notice them, others appear so fundamental that you may not dare do away with them; many so small that they seem hardly worthy a mention. But what if you hunted them out and changed them all? One a week. What would that unlock?

Ten years ago I was CEO of a London advertising

agency. At that time (and, to an extent, still) the creative director of an ad agency ruled the roost, and getting his or her 'sign-off' was a prerequisite for anything that was shown to the client. It was the thing that advertising agencies did and had in common. This wasn't considered a nice-to-have, it was considered sacrosanct and inviolable.

What, we wondered, would happen if, overnight, we did away with this rule, and instead allowed individual multidisciplinary teams to define their own processes? What if the 'sign-off' was stifling us and holding us back? It's easy to write now, but at the time it was a terrifying heresy. Yet we did it. And were transformed.

What are your equivalents?

The objective in freeing the sledge is shifting more of the team's everyday from the subconscious to the conscious. Doing this does not necessarily require a great effort or leap of imagination. If you have a regular meeting, hold it somewhere else, at a different time and different place. Invite different people. It's an example we could all do right now. In fact, even if you are not running a change programme this is a good idea. To be effective we need to be present and engaged, and regular shaking up of routine is a simple and effective way to keep us all fresh.

And remember, you can always change your mind. There are many routines I have blithely smashed away only to realise that there was a very good reason why it was as it was. On these occasions, we just switched back to how things had been previously. But even in doing this, we broke the casual acceptance of longstanding norms and habits, embedding instead a culture that questioned itself, asked why, was prepared to experiment, even fail, in search of new solutions. Even in these instances, the message to all became: there are no sacred cows, try it and see what happens.

3. Structures

Structures, job titles, hierarchies, committees and departments determine so much of how an organisation functions, and are necessary for it to work well. However, they also embed behaviours, culture, relationships and thinking. It is not necessary to be an iconoclast to wish to reset some or all of these structures. The simple addition (or removal) of one or two people from a particularly influential committee can be enough to create immediate change. The power of decisions like this are seen and understood by all. Changes such as this often result in significant resistance, but remember, overcoming sticking friction is why we're here.

Whatever your first step, it's unlikely to be the last team change you'll make, but it is of critical importance that you break the shape, patterns and habits of the team as it stood before. Before you can re-form it, you must break it, even if that too was a team you built – perhaps especially if it was a team you built. This was the genius of Sir Alex Ferguson, the iconic former Manchester United head coach: to be able to successfully build, break and rebuild.

Virtually everyone in all organisations is a member of a team. The leadership, structure, purpose, culture and objective of these teams shapes how they and, collectively, the whole organisation functions. These teams also set and maintain the routines that have become ingrained in the culture.

Much routine is shorthand, a way of getting the familiar done in an efficient and accepted way. To change these habits you must change how your teams work. Changing the cadence or location of meetings, clarifying (or re-orienting) their objective, duration or frequency – and in some cases simply cancelling them altogether – will demonstrate unequivocally that things aren't as they used to be. This breaking of structures and, therefore, routines also allows people around you to begin to understand the areas and behaviours you consider, even at this early stage, to matter the most.

There are, of course, far more dramatic interventions, from firing or reassigning people to the removal of roles and overturning of whole department structures. The time for this will come, but first you must quickly break habits and patterns with determined and clear action to begin to free the sledge.

4. Sensorium
The colour, design and layout of our environment has a dramatic effect on mood, behaviour and performance. Changing it is a relatively easy but very effective way to signal intent.

This is supported by a wealth of academic research. To pick but two of many:

'In clothing, interiors, landscape, and even natural light, a colour can change our mood from sad to happy, from confusion to intelligence, from fear to confidence.'

– Aves & Aves (1994)

'The design of an environment through a variety of means such as temperature, sounds, layout, lighting and colours can stimulate perceptual and emotional responses in consumers and affect their behaviour.'

– Kotler (1973) quoted in Yildirim,
Akalin-Baskaya and Hidayetoglu (2007)

I even happened across a Scandinavian study that showed that students performed better in a given task if they had a view of a pot plant rather than a magazine rack. You're welcome – I've done the reading so you don't have to.

Real hidden persuaders stuff, but humankind has known this for centuries. The great cathedrals were designed to awe and inspire their congregations; the purpose of a Japanese water garden is to bring serenity into our lives. In a modern office, low ceilings, loud noises, glare, poor air quality, uncomfortable temperatures and unpleasant smells are proven sources of stress and anxiety. All so obvious, they need no explanation.

In Chapter 1, we considered those factors that are within and without our control. In freeing the sledge we are concerned with those factors that are not only within our control, but where change can be quickly made. Sensorial changes to environment and context are very often easy and cheap to do, yet are frequently overlooked, not least because they fail to make it onto the Leadership Industrial Complex's list of activities 'suitable for grown-up leaders'. Serious leaders, however, get stuff done.

Some organisations consider the sensorial experience of their employees and clients as a matter of course. Supermarkets the world over pay great attention to this. In the UK, fresh fruit and veg are nearly always at the entrance. I can think of no example in Europe and the US where you enter the store to be confronted by the fish counter. However, when I visited a high-end supermarket in Shanghai, the store opened onto row upon row of tanks of live fish, crabs, lobsters – even frogs. Yet supermarkets in China and Europe have the same objective. In the UK, fresh veg is a shorthand for the freshness and quality of their goods; in China it is fresh (living) fish. First impressions matter.

Supermarkets also understand the other side of environment and context. It is a tough and competitive world, one where marginal pricing makes a huge difference to their market share and sales. Therefore, successful negotiations with major suppliers are a critical part of their business model. An executive from a major packaged goods company once described to me their experience of negotiating with a large supermarket chain. The meetings were held in a small, windowless room containing a hardwood table and uncomfortable chairs. Only water in a disposable plastic cup was offered. The mood was described as being like an interrogation room. If others dedicate so much time and attention to the topic, is it crazy if you do too?

In a team I once led, we built a completely glass-walled meeting room in the middle of the office to use for all our new prospect meetings. We wanted to create an effect of light, energy and movement. It was awkward to organise and seemed to many an unnecessary expense; 'What was wrong with all the other fabulous meeting rooms we had?' they argued. But it worked like a charm.

Why not try something similar by brewing real coffee in reception? We all do it when we're trying to sell our house, why not when we're trying to impress our clients or welcome our employees? Often, large buildings feel uninspiring because of their uniformity. Create radically different spaces within the building, spaces that look, feel, smell and sound different to each other:

- Welcoming and warm
- Quiet and studious
- Energetic and inspiring
- Communal and sociable.

It's not difficult to do. So get on and do it.

I once worked with a creative director who, at the end of a new business meeting, if it took place at the client's office, would waft the room with a scented joss stick called 'Sleepy Time' before the arrival of our competitor. I have no idea if it worked or not, but it still makes me laugh to think about it.

5. Embody the change you want to see

Physical actions matter. I often refer to the type of actions described above as making each Monday feel different to the preceding Friday. I like this because it suggests a continuous drive to signal change as a companion piece to larger, more strategic actions you plan to make or that are already underway.

The final piece is you. Ultimately, people must be persuaded to follow *you*. You must immediately set the tone and the pace of change. To be effective, you should consider how you plan to be the embodiment of the change you want to see.

This doesn't mean attempting to become somebody you're not, but it might mean pushing yourself out of your comfort zone, to challenge yourself to speak, act and behave in new or unfamiliar ways. You too may need to first examine, understand and then break some of your habits. Certainly this is not a business-as-usual situation, and therefore you, more than anybody else, cannot behave in a business-as-usual manner. This does not mean being inauthentic, but it does mean you should think carefully about how you use your behaviours to create the urgency and liberation of thought that you need going forward.

Justin Langer, the former coach of the Australian cricket team, tells a story of a lunch he had with one of his heroes, Sir Alex Ferguson, who we met a few pages earlier. The fiery Glaswegian was famous for his uncompromising style. No respecter of reputations, in anger he once kicked a boot across the dressing room with such force that David Beckham, who was the unintended recipient, required stiches above his eye. He memorably described his half-time dressing-downs as 'the hairdryer treatment'. An image that requires no elaboration.

Ferguson, however, knows a thing or two about leadership, egos and change, having created not just one championship-winning team but several over a period of two decades. He is one of the most successful football managers of all time. In the ultimate results business, for many, he remains the leader's leader.

Ferguson's advice to Langer was, 'the truth works'. It's a profound observation. It's not simply speaking your mind, it's describing a situation accurately, confronting difficulties, putting your hand up when you're wrong or unsure, when you're sad or happy, when you think things aren't as they should be. It is about being truthful without fear or favour.

The truth can be difficult and scary, but it doesn't have to lack empathy or compassion. It is possible to tell somebody something they really don't wish to hear in a way that enables them to come to terms with it and even grow and thrive as a result.

You can create change through how you communicate. Not simply what you say, but how and when you say it. You'll be surprised the effect this can have. People don't like bullshitters, so don't be one.

Urgent action builds confidence and belief

Freeing the sledge isn't primarily about movement, it is about the creation of collective energy, belief and confidence. For a leader and a leadership team, confidence isn't simply about winning or losing (because losing is an occupational hazard), it is about being in control. A confident team is one that feels it is in control of events, rather than events controlling them.

We began this chapter with an equation showing the relationship between change and action. We're going to end the chapter by exploring the relationship between confidence and action.

The confidence of an individual leader, and ultimately the team or organisation, is directly proportional to action taken. For the fellow maths geeks, it can be written as follows:

confidence $\propto$ action[*]

In simple terms, this means that if action doubles, confidence doubles; if action halves, confidence halves. The more you are able to impose your will on the situation through effective action rather than allowing the situation to dictate to you, the greater your confidence and self-belief and the greater the belief others will have in you.

It's an easy-to-observe and self-evident truth, one we see and experience every day. The opposite proves the point. There are few things more dispiriting and confidence sapping than working for a leader who appears unwilling or unable to act.

Yet this is a common position teams of all shapes and

---

[*] For the non-geeks, this means that confidence is directly proportional to action taken.

sizes find themselves in. They meet every week and find themselves discussing the same problems. Round and round they go: better and better at describing the problem, yet further and further from being prepared to act to solve it. It is amazing how quickly indecision destroys the confidence of a team and conversely how quickly action can build it up.

The consolation of action

Like being in a car accelerating from the lights, urgency is something you can feel; even with your eyes closed you know you're moving. Belief, then, is a quantity that you can readily build. You can build it through tiny, frequent steps. The determination to act will build belief in your ability to shape events. And shaping events is what change is all about.

You must believe that you can create change if you are to lead it. To free the sledge, you not only must build confidence through action; you must also be impatient. Not kick-the-doors down, tear-your-hair-out impatient, but impatient nevertheless. You must ask: by when, who will be responsible, what's our next step, why not now? You don't have to be *the* leader to do this, however; by being the motive force you become *a* leader. Don't leave a meeting without actions, don't start a meeting without an objective.

There's no better or more liberating feeling than getting that sledge slowly sliding forward. The time for thinking, if not over (there's always time for thinking), must now be paired with action. And action begets action.

The more you do, the faster you feel change happening, the greater your confidence to continue what will be a long and difficult journey.

Though those around you may not show it, they too will feel the change, the new energy and the release from old orthodoxies and habits. Some may mourn their passing, some may remain fearful, some may not like the direction you have chosen, but all will feel it and will begin their own process of change. Like flowers following rain in the desert, energy will appear where none existed before; people who had been written off or who were previously invisible will come to life. Ideas will come from places they never had before; you'll start to feel others walking at your side.

The crucial insight the leader must grasp when rebuilding a broken team or organisation is that initially the direction of travel matters less than the creation of belief that change is possible. At this stage, your destination is sufficiently distant to be far less important than the need to create the necessary energy and belief to free the sledge.

Don't allow your natural fear of being wrong deter you from action. In beginning change, urgent action is a prelude to direction. Be afraid of inaction. You must make your organisation, and yourself perhaps, believe that change is possible, and that change is happening. Right now. It proves that you're not just another doomed leader full of talk and empty on action, to be laughed at on the phone by Terri. You're different.

You're still a long way from the finish line, but now the sledge is moving, you're on your way. This is how change begins.

NO BULLSH*T BREAKING FREE

Change is a physical activity that doesn't begin until you act.
The leader's most immediate task is convincing their team that
change is not just desirable, but that it is going to happen.
And fast. That whatever else, tomorrow is going to be different
to today, that next week will be different to this week; that
they are not the latest in a long line doomed to fail.

Change impact = (direction + communication) x action

Many change programmes founder not for want of ideas and sincere intentions, but for want of effective, consistent and long-term action.

Sticking friction > kinetic friction

The energy required to get an object moving is *always* greater than the energy required to keep it in motion. So it is with change.

Initially, direction matters less than movement

Your first priority is to ensure everyone believes that change, any change, is possible, that it is anything but business as usual. It's going to happen, and it's going to happen fast.

Five powerful ways to free the sledge

1. Environmental change.
2. Break routines and habits.
3. Deconstruct and reconstruct organisational structures.
4. Sensorial change.
5. Most importantly, lead by example.

Confidence $\propto$ action

Confidence is proportional to action taken.

The more you are able to impose your will on the situation rather than allow the situation to dictate to you, the greater your confidence and self-belief, and the greater the belief others will have in you.

5

TEAMS

What unites successful leaders is their understanding that they cannot do it alone.
They need to find their First Five, build effective teams that endure and encourage the development of other great leaders throughout their organisation.

If I have seen further, it is by
standing on the shoulders of giants.
Sir Isaac Newton

Individual commitment to a group effort –
that is what makes a team work, a company work,
a society work, a civilisation work.
Vince Lombardi

A COMPELLING CASE CAN BE MADE that Dwight D. Eisenhower was the greatest and most important leader of the twentieth century. Ike, as he was universally known, was appointed Supreme Commander of the Allied Expeditionary Force in early 1944, tasked with leading the liberation of occupied Europe.

The D-Day landings remain the largest and most complex single military operation ever undertaken, a complexity that cannot be understood in numbers alone, although they are mind-boggling. By the conclusion of the war in Europe in May 1945, Eisenhower commanded 5.5 million men and women, 28,000 aircraft and 970,000 vehicles. These numbers tell only part of the story. Armies from eight nations took part in D-Day, all with their own egos, customs, doctrines, strengths, weaknesses and, of course, jealousies. Or, as General George Patton, one of Eisenhower's deputies, put it, 'God deliver us from our friends. We can handle the enemy.' It was Ike's leadership genius that held this coalition together through the long and gruelling eleven months from Normandy to VE Day.

By 1944, there were many very capable and proven battlefield commanders in the Allied ranks, and many more who firmly believed they were. Inter-service, inter-regiment and international rivalries were ingrained facts of Allied military life. For the men at the top (and they were all men), this was their career, chosen long before war began. Many actively sought advancement, were unafraid to use fair means or foul to achieve it and viewed the war's denouement as a once-in-a-lifetime opportunity. Many field commanders actively courted fame, and some even had their own PR teams who, operating not unlike modern spin doctors, would brief for their boss and covertly against their rivals.

In the eye of this storm stood Eisenhower, promoted in some cases above the heads of those once senior to him and tasked with the greatest and most important mission of his – arguably any – lifetime. There were undoubtedly other more competent soldier-generals, those who could better read the ebb and flow of modern battle, but there were none who possessed his coalition-building, political and leadership skills. No other who could see, feel and experience the mighty egos and, rather than wilt, mould them into a formidable and unified whole.

Eisenhower was an excellent judge of men, being prepared to overlook imperfection of character in return for appropriateness of capability. Brilliant at selecting the right person for the job, he was also ruthless enough to remove those who failed. He had the ability to see through the variations of personality to the individual's most core strength and enable him to maximise it for the benefit of the whole.

In total war, the line between politics and military strategy is blurred. As the face of the Allied military effort, Eisenhower also had to be a politician – he too had bosses. Churchill and Roosevelt were men unafraid (indeed in Churchill's case eager) to share their opinion on strategies. Stalin, an uncomfortable ally, twisted their tails. In democracies, governments must get re-elected, their citizens prepared to make sacrifice, but only if they believe that sacrifice to be proportional; that their blood and gold are expended with great care. All this also lay on Eisenhower's shoulders.

Eisenhower's record is unimpeachable. The coalition he built and maintained was one of daunting internal tensions but, ultimately, formidable strength. Never forgetting he headed a citizen army, one that was led by consent rather than coercion, he did more than simply hold the egos in check. He forged a mighty and unified fighting force, one able to perform feats of arms, logistics and after the war's end, political rebuilding, that are unmatched before or since.

Eisenhower was the right man for the most important job of the age. Even today we have reason to remain grateful for his ability to forge a team from the most complicated ingredients and prevail. He remains the only man in history for whom becoming US president is only the second greatest achievement of his life.

None of us will face the challenges Eisenhower faced. His objective was obvious, and he understood that his single most important task in achieving it was to build and maintain powerful and effective teams. Teams strong enough to contain men of vaulting ambition, huge egos and who bore terrible responsibility. Whatever their personal feelings toward each other, and at times these were toxic, he was utterly intolerant of behaviours that damaged the coherence of the whole and therefore that would undermine the mission. 'You can call him a son of a bitch,' he once chided a subordinate, 'but not a British son of a bitch.'

Brilliant teams everywhere

In this chapter, we will consider the three aspects of team building that you will need to lead effective change and achieve enduring success. Like much else concerned with change, these are unlikely to be consecutive activities; however, they are presented here in a deliberate order of priority:

1. First Five: a coalition for change
2. Building a high-performing organisation: aligning individuals with the collective
3. Effective leaders everywhere: the accelerant of change

1. First Five: a coalition for change

In leading change, time is not on your side. Whether pressured by customers, bosses, shareholders, owners, employees, the bottom line or, commonly, a combination of some or all of these, you need to move fast. To do so, your first and most important action is to build about you a coalition who will rapidly multiply your impact. The First Five is a very simple concept and sounds a familiar, even obvious idea, yet its importance is often overlooked. It is the kernel for all that will follow.

I have often spoken of the idea to groups of leaders around the world. If you regularly do presentations and speeches you begin to get a sense from the room of which points really hit home; people scribble notes or photograph the screen. This is invariably one of those moments.

Your First Five (or two or three or six) is a small, tight-knit group of people, ideally some of whom you already know and have worked with before, although that isn't a prerequisite. Above all else, you must trust each other implicitly. It is a group who you can be vulnerable with, who can help you problem-solve without fear or favour, who share your ambition and values, who will be honest with you and each other and, most importantly, who you know can deliver. It's more a gang than a conventional team.

It cannot simply be the people who through luck and circumstance you happen to find yourself surrounded with; they cannot be just any old group who you attempt to mould like reluctant clay. Those who you choose cannot be defined simply by job titles, seniority or experience, and especially not by politics. There's plenty of time for all that as you go (I'm not naïve to these demands), but not now.

Though not necessarily entirely comprised of the most senior people, some will need to be, and all will need the requisite seniority and experience to be able to get stuff done and directly impact the areas of the business you have initially identified as most in need of attention. They must all be proven, high-quality practitioners in their field, as they will help you lead change through doing. You may evolve and grow this group over time, but if you find them and find them fast they will catalyse your rate of change.

We see First Fives all the time in top-level sport. New managers brought into Premiership football clubs never come alone; they bring a small, tight and trusted team with them. This isn't laziness or jobs for the boys, it's a recognition that time is short, that change is a team sport, and that they need a multiplier effect right from the off. Giselle Mather, Director of Rugby at Wasps Rugby Club (who we met previously), describes each weekly team selection announcement as a cultural hand grenade. In an environment of such unrelenting pressure, where results are both immediate and unforgiving, the irresistible pressure of the fixture list means leaders simply do not have the luxury of starting completely from scratch. They need to come with an objective, a leadership philosophy and quickly assemble a core team who can begin to execute from day one.

First Five principles

The idea of a First Five resonates so strongly with people because it doesn't work like a traditional team; it is both looser and tighter, less formal and potentially more powerful.

- **Find them fast**

Your First Five are the team who, with you, will begin to free the sledge, so you need to prioritise finding them. Of course in the real world you cannot simply conjure up the right people, but you must put finding the first of them at the top of your to-do list. It will be time well spent.

- **Trust**

Trust is critical to the success of your First Five. You like each other, implicitly trust each other and always have each other's backs. If you've got this, you're well on your way.

- **Vulnerable and safe**

Change is difficult, demanding and sometimes lonely. The First Five is a safe space, where the whole is greater than the sum of the parts. It's a place where you can problem-solve, where doubts, fears and worries can be shared, eased and always listened to.

- **Great core skills**

This is the most basic and fundamental requirement. Ideally, their skill sets will be complementary, but don't think about this group in the way you would a normal team. They do not need to be able to do everything, but what they do, they need to do well.

- **Divide up tasks and lead through doing**

Whatever the opposite is of a talking shop, the First Five is it. This team is a team of doers. Getting stuff done is hard, but as we discovered in the previous chapter is the only way change happens. The First Five helps drive change through their core skills, their behaviours and getting their sleeves rolled up and doing it.

- **Frequently re-commit to each other**

Effective relationships, like a healthy garden, need love and nurture. It is easy to take close relationships such as these for granted. Don't. You must regularly meet, discuss, re-commit and share. Partly to ensure you retain your alignment (Chapter 3) and partly to ensure your interpersonal relationships remain strong. Don't assume everyone is OK.

- **Work hard**

Leading change is a demanding task. To succeed, you and your First Five will need to work hard in order to achieve your goals. This may be obvious, but you need those who are able and willing to take this on.

2. Building a high-performing organisation

An effective team is a group of individuals capable of achieving something none would be able to do on their own. To succeed, you must build powerful and thriving teams across your organisation.

Teams, because they are always made up of people, are difficult and complicated things. Every team has its own culture, be it good, bad, indifferent – or much worse.

We will consider the critical role of culture in more detail in Chapter 7, but in short, an effective culture is one that enables a team to achieve a level of performance that otherwise would be beyond it.

In order to build and sustain brilliant teams, it is important to understand individuals' relationship to their leader(s) and the organisation as a whole. This can be shown using the grid below.

- **Vertical axis: In my Interests**
  A rational assessment of what is best for an individual's career at a particular life stage. For example, the role may be well paid, it may provide opportunity for promotion, career advancement, specific training or experience.

- **Horizontal axis: Aligns with my values**
  The extent to which the role aligns with their personal values, is emotionally fulfilling and that they are engaged with the organisation's ambitions (and, in the context of change, yours).

Thriving, cruising, disconnected, stalled

Everyone sits somewhere on this grid, and they will move around over time depending on a range of factors, from salary, career ambitions and status to leadership, culture or the demands of relationships and family. It is impossible to distil the human condition to a single grid, but it's a useful tool and illustrates the change-leader's challenge when considering the motivations and performance of those in their teams. In general terms, you must strive to move people in the direction of the arrow shown, from bottom left to top right, though of course the vast majority exist in all the spaces in between these two extremes.

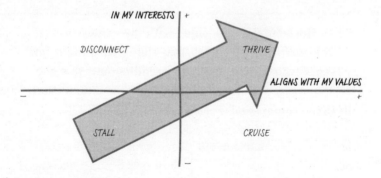

1. Thrive
People who are in the top-right quadrant believe that the fulfilment of the team ambition is fully aligned with the fulfilment of their own personal career ambitions. People here feel inspired by their leaders, the task at hand and

that they have control over their career and the choices they make. We want as many people as possible to be in this quadrant. People here feel that, on the whole, they are able to control events rather than events controlling them.

2. Cruise

People in the bottom-right quadrant typically are comfortable in their roles and like, even admire, the organisation. They may be very diligent and hard working, but are well within their personal comfort zone. Though they may feel valued, they are aware that they could achieve more, yet personal or organisational barriers are in the way. For many in this quadrant, work life is comfortable and familiar, but when it comes to making change there is little room for cruising, and consequently people here may feel particularly threatened by your programme.

You need to find compelling reasons for these people to fully re-engage and align their ambitions with yours. Having too many people in Cruise may be the very reason the organisation needs to change in the first place.

I once had a rather fractious conversation with a potential employer. 'I can see why it's in your interests to hire me, but I can't see why it's in my interests to take the role,' I observed, after several long and, in truth, interesting conversations. I think they thought it rather rude of me to be so blunt. However, it is a perfectly reasonable question. I didn't just want to know about how fabulous their organisation was, I wanted to know why it would be fabulous for me. It seemed to be something they hadn't really considered.

3. Disconnect

There are economic and other perfectly valid professional reasons for people to be in the top-left quadrant. I have called it Disconnect because here the individuals may work hard, may be valued and consider they get a good financial return for their effort, but have little love, passion or enthusiasm for their job or the organisation. They may even, at worst, be holding their nose to avoid the smell.

There are very good and compelling reasons why somebody may choose to do a job they do not love or even like, or why they might work for somebody they find uninspiring, unimpressive or worse. At its most positive, this is a choice the individual has made rather than a situation they find themselves in. However, it is obviously the case that there are many examples (perhaps more) of the latter.

4. Stall

Nobody wants to be here, however many are, particularly in failing teams. Here people are bored, underutilised, disenfranchised and demoralised. For any organisation they are essentially wasted resource. They exist on the spreadsheets of HR, payroll and the P&L, but you get from them only a fraction of what is possible.

First and foremost, this isn't their fault, it is yours.

Your task as a leader is to move as many people from the bottom left to the top right as possible. And then keep them there.

At different times in our career we might find ourselves in any one of the four boxes, though hopefully, not too often in the bottom left. We should also not assume that people are irrational actors – quite the opposite. Many choose to be in Disconnect or Cruise at different times (few choose to be in Stall).

If we are about to buy a house, we may happily tolerate being top left for a while in return for a higher salary or greater security. Many people of whom we might say, 'they stayed in that job too long', do so because they are in Cruise; it's not necessarily doing much for their career, but it's comfortable and familiar.

Nevertheless, in both cases, as leaders of change, we need people to feel the gravitational pull of the top right. Much of successful change can be simplified to increasing this pull and removing the barriers that inhibit movement, thus drawing more and more people into Thrive.

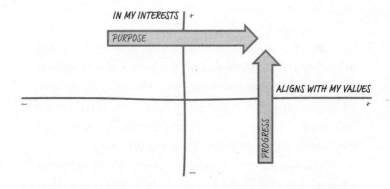

Ambitious people desire both purpose (a move to the right) and/or progress (a move upwards), as shown above. Smart organisations are not blind to this. Many of the more remunerative sectors (to avoid offence and stereotypes, I will allow you to decide who they are) commit huge amounts of money to community outreach programmes, CSR and other such activities because they recognise their employees' desire for purpose, but feel unable to provide it from within. I'm all for this, but it is rather like carbon offsetting: better than nothing, but imagine how much better it could be for their company, the employees' sense of emotional reward and society as a whole if this was baked in rather than simply bolted onto the side.

Then, of course, there's bottom left. Stalled. I can think of no good reason to be here, but I know I have been at various points in my career, and you may have been too. It's not terminal, but if you're here, you need to do something about it, even if that means just stepping out and spending time rethinking what you really want to do.

A mistake many leaders make, however, is to conclude that the people they find in Stall are here by choice, that it's their fault. This often is not the case. They are here because the organisation has allowed them to drift into this position, or even pushed them into it (as a result of a toxic culture, for example). For many companies, they represent their most wasted asset. It costs little if anything more to have somebody top right than it does bottom left, yet the difference in return between the two is enormous.

The individual's journey of change

In leading change, you should consider the concentration of individuals in the top-right quadrant as a defining part of your task. Inevitably, you will have people who are in different places across the grid, and this is a powerful way of imagining *their* journey.

Great change is the aggregation of many hundreds, perhaps thousands, of individuals breaking habits and being inspired to do the familiar in a new or different way. Ultimately, if all change happens at an individual level you also need to work hard to break your ambitions down to ensure they have meaning and relevance at that level also. Change is personal before it's collective.

We are all very good at identifying the things around us that we consider to be done badly, or people who don't cut it, or processes that could be improved. The problem is, not only does this not necessarily help, it can actively hinder. You don't want the response, 'Yeah, she's right, if only everybody else would buck their ideas up.' What you need is for people to spend very little time thinking about all the things everyone else could do better and instead to think only of the things that they themselves plan to do differently – from 'What are they going to do?' to 'What am I resolved to do?'

Don't hope people get the message; be explicit. When concluding a presentation that demands action, spell it out, leave no room for ambiguity. You need to cut through to the person who was thinking about last night's date or this morning's argument. Ask your audience to think right now, before they stand up and leave, what they are going to do. Just one thing, but one thing related to the task and that is wholly in their control. Just imagine how much would get done, so much more quickly, if everyone did that, and kept doing it. If you're going to succeed, then this must be the case eventually. So you might as well start now.

The more dysfunctional and broken your organisation, the more people you are likely to have toward the bottom left, stalled and stuck. The higher-performing it is, the more who will be in the top right; your task is to get as many there as possible. Obvious stuff. Depending on the nature of your task, the concentration of individuals in the Thrive quadrant can be either the objective or the enabler of your change programme. In a failing or moribund team, the leader's task can be easily understood and simply illustrated by the migration of individuals from the bottom left to the top right.

Transforming teams

This is a classic example of a virtuous circle. People who are thriving are more motivated, directed and effective. Consequently, they are likely to stay with you longer and be powerful advocates for others you wish to bring in, further strengthening the whole; the team will perform better, and with a wider dispersal of effective leaders throughout the organisation the more people will, in turn, be drawn into Thrive. Which will lead your organisation more effectively toward its goal. Furthermore, such an organisation is far more able to re-orient and change in response to the kind of internal and external challenges we considered in Chapter 1.

It is your ability to get as many people as possible into the top right that is a true measure of people's willingness to follow you, and why. This is why successfully leading change is rather more complicated than just being liked or being a nice person. There are plenty of people who work for 'nice guys' who are in the bottom of the bottom left box. Without effective leadership we all drift gradually to the bottom left, as sediment sinks in stationary water.

Bottom left to top right: migrating toward Thrive

Imagine going for a job interview where the person you met could tell you only one thing in order to persuade you to join. (Assume, for the purpose of the exercise, that the functional aspects of role – money, title, etc. – are taken care of.) What would it be?

In leading change it's not so hypothetical; in some senses change poses this question in reverse. The vast majority of the people you must connect with are not applying for a role; they are, however, evaluating their relationship with you. Are you Hugh Abbot, or something entirely different? And, dare they even hope, better. What would better even mean for them? This is the calculation your teams will make as you stand before them, and them before you. I long mulled these questions. Their solution is ultimately how you help move people toward Thrive, and the answer is both clarifying and uncomplicated.

Be great for the careers of those who work for you

Leaders who want individuals to stay and thrive, and teams that outperform, must find answers to one critical challenge. They must be great for the careers of those who work for them. It's a high bar. This does not mean only great for those who stay with them, but those who thrive with them, who thrive after them and who ultimately thrive beyond them.

In my idealised job interview, I would want to know only one thing: will they be great for my career? It is the ultimate expression of change on the individual level: getting from where I am now to a better point in the future, one that aligns with my functional aspiration and my values.

From Disconnect to Thrive (purpose)

In Disconnect, the individuals may work hard, be valued and consider they get a reasonable return for their effort. This could most obviously be financial, but could also be related to status, job security, opportunity for rapid advancement, training, attainment of professional qualifications and so on. However, they have little love, passion or enthusiasm for the organisation and in many cases their job; it is simply a means to their own end. Some may consider this to be enough; others only tolerate their position. However, their lack of engagement with the collective and focus on individual position and/or status makes them a missed opportunity and at worst a barrier to your change programme.

Those who work only for a functional benefit lack emotional engagement with their role and the organisation as a whole. They are there solely for them, which is fine up to a point. But great organisations need great teams and effective cultures, a combination of the individual and the collective. In leading change, you require a high degree of engagement from the majority: they must believe in your mission, your vision and your strategies. You need people to see the personal benefit that lies in collective achievement. This is the journey from Disconnect to Thrive.

Disconnect to Thrive can be considered as re-balancing an individual's perspective of their role in the organisation, **from the individual toward the collective**.

Disconnect → Thrive (purpose) example actions you can take

- **Quantitative** employee surveys to understand levels of comprehension, engagement and overall satisfaction with the organisation or team vision.
- **Qualitative** surveys to expand on the above. As discussed in Chapter 1, these can be used for far more than simply listening.
- Be clear that your ambition sees no conflict between **value and values**, that both are necessary for your organisation to thrive. There is no need to have to make a choice.
- Ensure you have been consistently clear in your **communication (Chapter 2)** on the organisation's societal role and cultural ambitions.

- Emphasise the centrality of effective teams to the organisation's future success.
- Ensure you walk the walk regarding the desired **cultural behaviours (Chapter 7)**. For example, the establishment of **KPIs that are shared throughout the organisation** that cover a range of indicators beyond the purely functional. All come with both targets and progress markers.
- Identify the most important and influential individuals in Disconnect and **build personal development** plans to give them active roles in your programme.
- Identify key individuals who may be **blockers**, delivering results (for you and themselves) but who will not or cannot align their behaviours with the desired culture. Ultimately, if you cannot convert these people, you may need to remove them (see **Jack Welsh's Grid in Chapter 7: Culture**).

From Cruise to Thrive (progress)

People in Cruise are generally quite content. Their role suits them, they know what they're doing and they are familiar with their surroundings. They may have been at the organisation for some time, long enough to know its foibles, its strengths and weaknesses, how it thinks, what it likes and dislikes, and how to get their job done with the minimum of fuss. Some are frogs in warming water, but this implies a degree of ignorance or even denial about their circumstance. This is not always the case. For some it is simply that the circumstance suits them; they maybe would like to do something about it. But not today.

- Many people here may like the organisation, but are stuck in its routines, its habits and its behaviours. They would perhaps like it to perform better, but that desire is out-weighed by their fear that change may destroy their comfortable and familiar world. They have a high level of organisational engagement, but often with the existing order and therefore may be barriers to your programme. Ultimately many here prefer everything as it is, warts and all.
- Cruise to Thrive can be considered as re-balancing an individual's perspective of their role in the organisation as **from the collective toward the individual**.

Cruise → Thrive (progress) example actions you can take

- **Quantitative** employee surveys to understand levels of comprehension and belief that your programme will deliver positive individual benefits (such as better training, better pay or improved prospects for promotion), as well as understanding levels of anxiety that exist around it.
- **Qualitative** surveys to understand resistance, fears and questions regarding your vision. As discussed in Chapter 1, these can be used for far more than simply listening.
- Be clear that a thriving organisation provides fresh

opportunity for all, opportunities to fulfil personal as well as collective ambitions.

- Ensure you have been consistently clear in your **communication (Chapter 2)** that nobody will be left behind, that you do not intend to throw the baby out with the bathwater, that you value existing knowledge and experience, that you need great leaders everywhere.
- Identify key individuals and **build personal development** plans to give them active roles in your programme.
- Demonstrate through your behaviours that a thriving organisation provides opportunities not previously available – and that you plan to run a meritocracy. The best will rise to the top. **Build clear pathways that all can see**. For example: refresh influential leadership groups and teams; invest in coaching for individuals you consider to have untapped potential; develop next generation leadership schemes.

3. Effective leaders everywhere: the accelerant of change

What unites great leaders is the understanding that they cannot do it alone, that they too need great leaders for their programme to succeed. The identification and development of leadership talent is key to leading change. Though this is obvious, in practice many organisations fail to take the development of their leaders seriously, not least because they misunderstand what leadership is.

In the same way that you can consider change to be the accumulation of as many people as possible in Thrive, so too you should actively consider the identification and development of leadership talent as a key part of your programme. Great leaders, at all levels, create a positive cycle of improvement, talent attraction, cultural change, talent retention and further performance improvement. It is therefore possible to gain active competitive advantage through doing this well, not least because so few do. Stretch people, treat them like adults, push their careers forward, shove them into the top right. Some may stumble, but those who thrive are worth double. Leadership is difficult but not complicated, and like any other skill it can be learnt, so set about enabling people to do just that.

This is a primary task for the First Five: who and where are the next advocate-leaders? As with all other aspects of change, the most effective way to achieve forward momentum is to focus on the positive rather than the negative, those most able and willing to help, rather than fretting over those likely to get in the way. The selection and development of effective allies is far more powerful in moving your programme forward than the drag of the naysayers.

You must quickly make an assessment of the leadership strength of the organisation you are responsible for. Obviously, the likely answers to this question will look very different in a high-performing team than it will in a low-performing one, but it is a critical exercise nevertheless, and though potentially time consuming, it is time well spent; there is always lots of room for improvement. Honesty, here, is an indispensable ally.

Because in leading change time is not on your side, I have outlined below a simple and quick approach that will give you a clear baseline for your organisation's leadership potential and, once you have it, a plan for how to proceed.

Assess

Identify those already in important leadership roles and assess their current performance against the following four criteria:

1. Results

Leadership is a results business. If they are delivering against their objectives then it's a great start. If they aren't, it's important to find out why. For example, are they clear what their objectives are?

2. Cultural alignment

Do they exhibit the behaviours you believe define the future organisational culture (see Chapter 7). If not, do you think they can, and will, change?

3. Team

How effective are the teams they run? And why? An effective, well-run team is a sure marker of a leader who is doing an awful lot right.

4. Talent
How strong is the calibre of people who work for them? A strong team that contains great people is a powerful signifier of effective leadership.

Here, confirmation bias can sometimes lead you astray. First impressions matter, but they are not always a reliable guide. Often, I have seen examples where effective and potentially valuable people have been pulled adrift, forced out or even fired because their face didn't fit. And similarly, those good at playing the game but little else, remain. If you want to make fast progress, it's in your interests to make sure this doesn't happen.

This four-point checklist provides hard metrics to help you make clear-eyed decisions, as well as giving the individuals themselves every opportunity to become integral to your programme. If they don't want to, then ultimately, one of you needs to decide that they must go.

Investing in leadership

Great and effective leadership always involves other people, often people you don't know very well, and sometimes great numbers of people who you have not met and likely never will. Perhaps one of the reasons there is so much mysticism around the subject is this ability of effective leaders to impact, enthuse, motivate and inspire people who they don't know and who are very different to them.

You and your First Five must quickly build a programme, perhaps a number of programmes depending on size, to develop a long-term culture of high-performance leadership. It is the surest investment you can make for the development and future health of your organisation. It should be close to the top of your list, and though many organisations say they do it, few do it well. Therefore, the opportunity for competitive advantage by building a programme that your employees are eager to join, your customers value and your competitors envy is significant.

A simple but effective leadership development programme

1. An integrated approach

Many organisations invest in leadership, but do it piece-meal. Instead, you should take a single, integrated approach. Leaders at different levels will access the programme at different points; employees will work their way up it as they progress.

This approach has four important benefits that strengthen and deepen your organisation's leadership capability:

i. It embeds understanding of your organisation's leadership philosophy: what it is, why it matters and how to do it well.

ii. It engenders cumulative learning. Each step builds on the last.

iii. It creates a culture of aspiration and retention. A programme that has real and tangible career benefits will aid retention and attraction of talent.

iv. It embeds a shared leadership language across the organisation.

2. Make it somebody's job

If it's going to get done and done well, it needs to be close to the top of somebody's to-do list. Reduce other programmes to find space and funding to do this well. Everything else flows from effective leadership.

3. Agree metrics

So much that is spent on training and development is wasted for want of clear alignment with the organisation's priorities and clear success criteria. You need to understand which parts of your leadership programme are working and which are not. Agree some metrics (for example, retention of the brightest talent, rates of promotion of the course's alumni, and staff engagement scores) as well as asking for frequent feedback from its participants. Align at least some of the programme's metrics (KPIs) with those of the organisation as a whole.

Leadership isn't a separate activity. It *is* the activity.

4. A sample four-tier programme

Don't overcomplicate it; for example, you could consider four tiers:

i. C-Suite Executives

An individualised programme including coaching and externally accredited partners to build a best-in-class senior leadership programme. Partner with a leading business school to do so.

ii. Senior Leaders

An accelerator programme designed to prepare people for executive-level roles.

iii. High Fliers

Mid-level executives identified as the organisation's future leaders. This internal and/or externally led mini MBA programme will accelerate growth and aid retention of this critical group.

iv. Next Gen

A programme to identify and accelerate the development of your junior leaders.

5. Exclusivity drives aspiration and value

Places on the programme should be valued and not just come by right. It is possible to create a virtuous circle of exclusivity driving perceived value. The greater the competition for places, the stronger your leadership base.

The Matthew effect

There is a rubric, beloved of Silicon Valley, known as the Matthew effect. It is derived from a verse in the Bible:

'For unto every one that hath shall be given, and he shall have abundance: but from him that hath not shall be taken away even that which he hath.'

– Matthew 25:29 (KJV)

The Matthew effect describes the idea of accumulated advantage: those who start ahead gain continued benefit from having done so. It has been applied to many areas of life, including the accumulation of capital, fame and status.

It applies also to talent in your organisation. As that great and misunderstood Florentine sage Niccolò Machiavelli noted 1,400 years after Matthew, 'The first measure of the intelligence of a ruler is the quality of the men he has around him.' The surest way for you to get great talent into your team is through having great leaders in your team. Great leaders beget great leaders, great talent attracts great talent. You want more than your fair share of both. However, as we know, it's not easy; progress demands consistent and determined effort. But an organisation that successfully invests in great leadership at all levels and has a programme to migrate and maintain as many employees as possible into Thrive will win far more than it loses.

Who among us wouldn't want to work there?

Naysayers

John Kotter, of Harvard Business School, a great guru of organisational change, wrote a book on the subject in the manner of a children's story called *Our Iceberg Is Melting*. It has the gift of brevity and is a smart idea, his argument being that too many books about change are just too dull to get through. I couldn't agree more.

In *Our Iceberg Is Melting*, he describes a penguin colony faced with the melting of their iceberg home and wrestling with how to change in response. Its most memorable aspect is that the format allows him to sketch each character, Fred, Alice, Louis, Buddy, the Professor and NoNo, as archetypes familiar to us all. The story is of crisis, heroic action, resistance and, of course, redemption.

I once, many years ago, when tasked with what seemed an unfixable team, bought five copies of the book and handed them round. I deliberately bought too few and asked each member, having read it, to leave their name inside the cover and then pass it on. It was a neat little exercise in symbolism and collectivity. As I watched the list of names grow and the covers become more tattered, one penguin stood out.

Poor old NoNo's nominative determinism means his role in the story needs little explanation, but for my team he became the talking point. Briefly he became shorthand for naysayers of all shades. Amongst teasing and laughter, people speculated who our NoNo was (or were). In all teams there are those for whom the resistance to change is innate.

NoNo: triage, ignore, convert, cauterise

I'm not a business school professor and have a very pragmatic approach to those who stubbornly resist. This stems in part from the leadership equation introduced in Chapter 4:

impact = clarity x action
If action = 0 then change doesn't happen

For this reason, those who resist change have the potential to be an existential threat to those tasked with leading it. Teams intuitively understand this, hence NoNo's brief anti-hero status. Stasis and change are incompatible. And if you're the leader and your programme fails, then you've failed. So you need a plan.

1. Triage
Identify the most stubborn areas of resistance and establish their importance to your mission, or more specifically the level of threat their non-alignment poses. For example, if it's the finance director or COO you have a pretty big problem; other roles may be important but are less likely to derail. Address the challenges in order of priority. It's always tempting to try to fix everything at the same time. Don't.

2. Ignore
Your motivating principle should be to move at the pace of the fastest. Where possible, those who resist should be treated like a rock in a stream; the water will flow round them. Many, as with NoNo in Kotter's fairy tale, will gradually catch up. Some may not, but most (though not all) of those who don't will rapidly become irrelevant to your programme as it moves beyond them.

3. Convert
I once worked with someone who described a colleague as being in the tent, pissing in. We all know

them; active detractors are no laughing matter, and can be corrosive to your plans and team morale. If you deem them to be important actors, then you need to understand their concerns, some of which may be reasonable, and form a view over time on whether these can be addressed. These people may be in any one of the three suboptimal quadrants we identified earlier – Stall, Disconnect or Cruise – and the steps outlined earlier are applicable here. You must help them understand the eventual benefits for them personally, even if the process is uncomfortable or difficult in the short term.

Not everyone moves at the same speed; not everyone sees things as you do. Here, sometimes, patience can be a virtue (not something I often say). In a team that has a clear vision and real change momentum, many will gradually move from active detractor to advocate as a tail pursues a comet.

If these people are key to the running of the organisation then you ultimately need them as part of your coalition. If they remain outside they will remain at best an anchor and at worst a wrecker.

4. Cauterise
There may be some people who will never be reconciled with you, your team or your programme. If these people hold key roles then ultimately the only realistic solution, for you and them, is that they go elsewhere. They may be persuaded of this by you, may reach this conclusion themselves or it may be

a very messy divorce. But leading change is difficult enough without your biggest fights being with your own team. Eventually, enough will be enough. Once you know, get on with it.

Ultimately, your success will be built upon effective, motivated teams

Successful change is a team sport. First you must build a tight coalition around you, your First Five. With this group you agree your initial objectives, divide up priority tasks, lead through doing and begin to mould yourselves and then others into a tight-knit and effective team. Ultimately, a culture of great, well-led teams is the surest way to achieve and sustain success.

Effective teams are powerful and self-supporting entities capable of moving fast and changing direction quickly. Their creation should not be left to chance but should be a deliberate and careful process, one that is more art than science, but is the ultimate task of all leaders. This is why the identification and development of effective, motivated leaders throughout your organisation is so important. Great leaders have a greater percentage of their people in Thrive, which is why their teams outperform. You can't succeed without them.

NO BULLSH*T TEAMS

What unites successful leaders is their understanding that
they cannot do it alone.
They need to find their First Five, build effective teams
that endure and encourage the development of other great leaders
throughout their organisation.

Find your First Five

Your First Five are a small, tight-knit group who you trust implicitly,
who you can be vulnerable with, who you can problem-solve with
without fear or favour, who share your ambition and values, who
will be honest with you and each other and, most importantly, who
you know can deliver.

Find them fast.

They must be people you trust and who trust you.

Create an environment where you feel safe with each other.

They must have great core skills.

Divide up responsibilities and lead through doing.

Frequently re-commit to each other.

Be prepared to work hard.

Thriving, cruising, disconnected, stalled

Much of successful change can be simplified to increasing the pull
of the top-right quadrant of the grid (Thrive) and removing the
barriers that inhibit people's movement towards it.

In leading change, you should consider the concentration of individuals in the top-right quadrant as a defining part of your task.

Be great for the careers of those who work for you

With you, after you and beyond you.

Build great leaders everywhere

Great leaders, at all levels, create a positive cycle of improvement, talent attraction, cultural change, talent retention and further performance improvement. Gain active competitive advantage through doing this well.

Assessing leaders

- **Results:** Do they deliver?
- **Culture:** Do their behaviours enhance the culture?
- **Team:** Do they run strong teams?
- **Talent:** Can they attract and retain great people?

A simple and effective leadership development programme

Take an integrated, organisation-wide approach.
Make it someone's job.
Agree metrics in order to learn and develop.
Implement a unified programme from top to bottom.
Exclusivity drives aspiration and value.

Naysayers

Triage.
Ignore.
Convert.
Cauterise.

6

SCHWERPUNKT

How do you decide where to begin? Attempting to do everything
results in achieving nothing. Focusing on the point of maximum effect
(the *schwerpunkt*) is how you break free and move rapidly
towards your goal.

The sun's rays do not burn until brought to a focus.
Alexander Graham Bell

I don't focus on what I'm up against. I focus on my goals and I try to ignore the rest.
Venus Williams

At the end of the Napoleonic Wars in the early nineteenth century a Prussian general, Carl von Clausewitz, wrote a seminal work on military strategy entitled *Vom Kriege* (*On War*). It is a rather long and turgid tome, but has within it a number of revolutionary ideas. It is now considered the first modern work on military strategy. So influential does it remain that his thinking is routinely taught not just in military academies, but in business schools around the world to this day.

The central thesis of Von Clausewitz's thinking was the concept of *Schwerpunkt*, the point of greatest pressure, or maximum effort. In a nineteenth-century military world, where armies would form up in great opposing lines (at the time of the Napoleonic Wars these could be several miles long) and blast away at each other, *Schwerpunkt* was a revolutionary idea. Great generals of the past had previously considered the idea, but Von Clausewitz was the first to describe and codify it.

At its heart, like all great ideas, lies simplicity. Von Clausewitz argued that, rather than spreading their forces evenly along the battle front, pushing equally hard at every point, generals should focus their effort at one specific point, to position the mass of their force at a place of their choosing. This may be based on a perceived weakness of their opponent's line, a place where they have a geographical advantage, or for the tactical exploitation of a situation that emerges through the course of the battle.

In battles such as these, where great forces are arrayed against each other in mostly static positions, the general's objective is to break through their opponent's line and out into the open land behind. This was the aim of the titanic battles of the First World War (but not achieved by either side until 1918) and of General Eisenhower in Normandy. Once through their enemy's line, the cavalry (in the early 1800s) or the tanks (in the 1940s) could wreak havoc, able to destroy their opponents as they broke in disarray. The battle all but won. A successfully executed *Schwerpunkt* is a decisive move for generals and leaders of change alike.

If everything's broken, where do you begin?

I recently took a call from a newly promoted CEO. She'd done the fun bit: the press releases, the pay rise, the company meetings, the rounds of applause and occasional bouquet. She'd made a couple of big hires and had taken the formation of her leadership team seriously. They'd all now had a couple of months to get to know each other, their new positions and the dynamics of the business. But reality had begun to bite. They had the titles and the authority, but also the responsibility, and the problems were now all theirs. What on earth were they now actually going to do? Where should she start?

She knew (as nearly everyone does) roughly where she wanted to get to. As we've established, this is very important, but relatively easy, and after six months in the role she was well versed with all that needed doing. She and her team were working very hard, and they cared deeply about the task in hand. However, for all their fire and fury they had covered almost none of the ground between baseline and objective. I listened to her talk and was reminded of those scenes in horror films where the unfortunate protagonists walk all day through the forest only to find themselves passing the same crooked tree they had camped beneath the night before.

She had, she felt, done all the sensible things right. But despite that, nothing important seemed to change. They continued to struggle to find new customers, they lost money on those they already had, their product was ordinary and her team was ambitious but fractious. Most debilitating of all, she was still too busy fighting fires to do much of anything else.

Her challenge, and that for all leaders of change, is where on earth should she begin?

Schwerpunkt is a fundamentally simple concept to

understand, but done well it is how you effect change and change fast. Like my despairing client, you too want to break out of the grinding stalemate and into the clear green fields beyond, where you can accelerate toward your goal. Deciding upon and executing your *schwerpunkt* is where you start. You don't need to be able to pronounce it, but if you use it well it'll turbo-charge your progress. It does, though, I advised her, require clarity of thought, determination and a strong will to make it work.

Finding the time to change

The great challenges with attempting to change an organisation, whether one that is failing and needs to pick itself up from its knees, or one that is high-performing but needs to alter direction, are: lack of time, constrained resources and, consequently, the difficulty of finding space to think rather than simply react.

It is easy in books or at business schools to lay out the simple principles of change. I've done it here. They really are quite straightforward. The problem, as always, is that carrying them out is very difficult.

This is especially the case when it comes to a broken business; leaders find themselves swamped with a seemingly unending list of problems and crises. They get up at 6 a.m. and work until 8 p.m. They're tired. It's draining. Customers, bosses and employees demand their time. They are dragged hither and thither, working harder and harder, not just failing to progress, but perpetual victims of circumstance, unable to take control of events. The harder they work, the deeper the hole seems to become, the urgent so pressing that there is never the time or energy for the important. This is the situation my client found herself in.

Recognising the factors that you can control

There is a famous legend of the Danish King of England, Cnut (careful with the pronunciation). His name, even a thousand years on, is still used to describe those who are blind to the limits of their power. The story has it that, after a protracted and bloody struggle to win the crown, such was his sense of divine authority that he set his throne on the shore and forbade even the tides to approach him. 'I command you not to rise onto my land, nor presume to wet the clothing or limbs of your master,' he thundered.

Cnut has, however, been mischaracterised. Rather, as the spume began to dampen his robes he was making the opposite point to his sycophantic courtiers. There was that which he could control, and that which even he could not.

An effective leader of change has no more control over the tides, winds and currents than any other, but is able to take effective control of their circumstances. Leaders must be able to successfully navigate toward their goal despite the continual suck and draw of external forces – or indeed internal forces. It is this, more than any other single factor, that will determine whether your programme will succeed.

There is no task that is more important than you

Books can be hyperbolic; authors make an extreme case to allow themselves the rug-pull reveal of their uncomplicated solution. It's a strategy not without risk for the author who wishes to make a difference. You may read my example above and recognise some, but not all of it. Your situation, you tell yourself, is difficult, but it's not the disaster zone described – it's not *The Blair Witch Project*. You do sometimes have the opportunity to raise your head and look into the future; you do from time to time meet as a team.

But if you want to succeed, sometimes is not enough. Fixing the organisation you run does not require you and your team to work harder; dare I say, maybe you need to work less hard. It is just as difficult running a poor team as a great team. The difference is, the latter is so much more enjoyable and rewarding. To get there, however, you have to put your organisation first; you have to treat yourselves as your most important customer.

This is another of those things I say frequently to CEOs, and they always nod: of course. But many of those who nod *don't* put their organisation first – not because they don't care, but because the incessant demands of a team creaking at the seams never seems to allow them the luxury (as they see it) to do anything but fight fires.

Change favours the brave

Many of us progress through our careers by learning to be good firefighters. We become increasingly adept at spotting the glowing embers and jumping on them, beating them out before they can take hold. When, occasionally, a conflagration erupts, we throw ourselves at it, sweating the evenings and weekends until it's extinguished. It is undoubtedly an important skill to have. It also gives a great deal of satisfaction – who could deny that a firefighter is a critical worker? And we learn it's good for our careers. Useful, hard-working people get promoted, and rightly so.

But it's a habit you now have to break. You can't be only a firefighter if you're going to lead change. You have to find the time to focus on the next, not simply the now.

In Chapter 4, we learned to break free of our routines and habits in order to create the time and space for new ones to form. Finding time does not mean working harder. It means having the courage, the strength and the will to stop doing a significant amount that currently consumes your day and using that time to build something completely new.

If you are serious about change, then incrementalism doesn't work

Imagine the organisation you wish to change is represented as a graphic equaliser, perhaps like those on the stack systems beloved of 1980s music fans or found in recording studios today. There, each of the sliders controls the prominence of a specific wavelength of sound or instrument in the overall mix. By adjusting each one you arrive at your desired overall effect.

In your organisation, each slider represents an aspect

of the business you believe must be improved or even rev-
olutionised in order to achieve your goal. The majority of
leaders will find themselves in this position, faced by any
number of significant challenges, all with an equally good
case for immediate attention, all of which draw down on
their team's resources. Often, teams divide responsibility
for such tasks without much clear strategic thought; they
are done that way because that's how they've always
been done.

If, in seeking to tune the sound-mix to your taste, you
simply edge every slider forward by 1 per cent, it is likely
few but the most trained ears will notice. Indeed, the
overall mix will be unchanged, as each slider will remain
in the same position relative to the others. If instead you
imagine moving just one slide from the bottom to the
very top, leaving the others as they were, even the most
tin-eared will discern the difference. The challenge is to
decide which slide to move for the most immediate overall
effect. If you are serious about change, then incrementalism doesn't work. This is the *schwerpunkt*.

Change everything: change nothing

To achieve transformation there will be many tasks
demanding your attention, each with their advocates. The
temptation for change leaders, indeed often the reflex, is
to simply throw themselves into trying to fix everything.

The problem is, no matter their energy and effort, this
doesn't work, and such an approach dooms many ambitious leaders to failure. It is the equivalent of moving all

the slides forward by 1 per cent. Of course, they'd like to move them by more, but in practical terms, constrained by time and resources, this is impossible. By attempting to focus everywhere they focus nowhere. By attempting to change everything, they change nothing.

There is a compelling case for incrementalism at a later stage of the journey, perhaps as best exemplified by Sir Dave Brailsford's philosophy of incremental gains with the all-conquering British Olympic Cycling Team, but it is important to remember that this reached its apogee in a team that was already at the absolute peak of its performance. At this early stage, you need large, decisive movements, not baby steps.

Furthermore, this isn't simply lack of thought, care or attention on their behalf. Many of these challenges do need to be addressed, and various of their stakeholders, not least their bosses, often demand action. It is a difficult balance to strike. But strike it you must.

The alchemy of change: achieving more with the same

There would have been no need for Von Clausewitz to have written his book if there were no practical constraints on the armies he led. If he had unlimited time and unlimited manpower, then there would be no need for strategy and tactics. Victory would be inevitable.

Likewise, the reason leadership in general, and change in particular, is so damn difficult is because it asks the person in charge to achieve greater results from an essentially unchanged pool of resources, an alchemical effect, turning base metal to gold.

Of course you can alter some of the pieces on the board, hire a new general, raise a new regiment, change the managing director, make an acquisition, but all leaders are united in the central nature of their task, how they achieve a better outcome without more resources. Resources (money and time) are always constrained. If they weren't there would be little skill required.

It is this dual pressure of constrained resource and heightened expectation that make *Schwerpunkt* so critical to your success.

Breaking through

In established markets, the leading brands attempt to maintain their position by blocking out those who would seek to steal their crown, just as the canopy of the rain-forest stifles fresh growth below. In some sectors this has been achieved and maintained with considerable success for decades, Coca-Cola and McDonald's being familiar examples.

Companies such as these are, first and foremost, very good at what they do. Market-leading brands will typi-cally attempt to define and own the values and language of their entire category, thus, by forcing everybody else to play by their rules, making it far easier for them to maintain their pre-eminence.

McDonald's, through decades of successful product innovation (the food, but also store locations, service levels and so on) and marketing, has shaped our under-standing of what a great fast-food restaurant should be. And guess what – it's them. In many categories such as these, well over 50 per cent of the market is held by just two or three dominant brands, with a comet's-tail of others left to scrap over what's left. We see it in laundry, soft drinks, toilet tissues, razors and many more.

These brand leaders sit across their categories like great Napoleonic armies, their enormous lines attempting to block off every possible avenue a competitor may take in order to gain a foothold. For a challenger to simply line up opposite and batter their way past the leader is impossible; the barriers to entry are too high, and the anaconda-like dominant players will squeeze the life from them.

Those that succeed recognise that their large oppo-nents, by spreading themselves across the whole category, are vulnerable to a well thought-out and focused attack aimed at a specific point in the line, a point of their choosing – their *schwerpunkt*.

Colgate defined and dominated the toothpaste market, but Sensodyne, by focusing very tightly on what was initially a tiny niche (sensitivity), managed to carve out a huge global market for themselves. Colgate remain number one overall, but they are almost entirely absent from the sensitivity category that Sensodyne now owns, and where there is a significant price premium. Focusing tightly on one specific aspect of the whole category has enabled Sensodyne to become the second-largest tooth-paste brand in the UK.

Andrex and Gillette, both longstanding and dominant brand leaders, have recently been attacked by brands each using the same focal point, their sales model. Maintaining a high share of shelf space in supermarkets has always been a critical objective for brand leaders, effectively blocking out the competition. Both brands have been disrupted by competitors that have by-passed this channel and focused on selling direct, relying on subscription models to provide significantly lower price points and convenience to their customers with huge success, and consequently redefining the dynamics of two very established categories.

The greatest current example of the power of a well-executed *Schwerpunkt*, however, is in the automotive sector. The global car market is huge and dominated by a relatively small number of manufacturers. Over many years, cut-throat competition has driven down prices while heightened customer expectations and regulation has driven up the costs of manufacture. As a result, car makers have been forced into a series of mergers to achieve economies of scale. It has become harder and harder to produce money-making cars and, as the companies grew larger and larger, seemingly impossible to enter the market.

If all that wasn't bad enough, the industry has known for many years that the heart of their product, the internal combustion engine, is a big problem. As every school child knows, they create short-term air quality problems and contribute significantly to climate change. The car companies need to switch to electric, but that is easier said than done. And very, very expensive. Consequently, most opted to talk a lot about it, but to kick the can down the road. Like the valve manufacturers of the 1960s, they saw it coming, but were unwilling or unable to act.

Richard Branson once said that the quickest way to become a millionaire was to start out as a billionaire and launch an airline. The same now surely applied to the motor industry.

From launch in 2003, Tesla went all in on electric, but at the time there were almost no public charging points, buyers were nervous about the new technology, the cars were expensive, they didn't have showrooms and were available in very few colours with almost no optional extras. They appeared to be at best a west coast fad, at worst a billionaire's vanity project. However, like Sensodyne, Tesla knew what they were and what they weren't. They weren't interested in taking on the massed lines arrayed in front of them; instead they fought on a very narrow front, on territory unfamiliar and difficult for the established multinationals. At first, so difficult was it for the major manufacturers to respond, they hardly tried. Tesla seemed unlikely to survive, and if they did they would surely remain a small player.

However, it turned out that significant numbers of people were prepared to buy electric if the product and brand were right, and that having no showrooms, no salesmen and few variants was, to many buyers, a plus, not a minus. It is a classic *Schwerpunkt*. The established manufacturers had the technology, they even had a few products, but for them it was just one of many things on their growing to-do lists. They were locked in their familiar battles with familiar foes and saw neither the opportunity nor the threat.

As Von Clausewitz had urged, Tesla's narrow and focused attack had enabled their cavalry to crash out into the wide, empty, green fields beyond. It is estimated that in the US Tesla now has a massive 75 per cent of the electric car market, the sector where all the growth is, and at the time of writing, with a market capitalisation of $930 billion, they are the sixth most valuable company in the world. For reference, the next most valuable car company is Toyota, at $200 billion, while the once mighty Ford Motor Company languishes at $62 billion.

Making *Schwerpunkt* work

To lead change, you need to be focused and deliberate in deciding your actions. Tackling everything at once will fail to move you toward your objective. However, fires will continue to smoulder away, demanding your attention, so you need to find an effective balance between the short term and the long. Deciding upon and executing your *Schwerpunkt* is the most effective way to move forward, but doing it well requires of you and your team much that we have covered so far; clarity of objective, alignment and mutual support will help you stay on track as events beyond your control attempt to pull you from your path.

1. A clear objective
By this point you know what this is. It should be clear, bold and ambitious, as we covered in Chapter 3.

Remember, *Schwerpunkt* is the means to the end, not the end in itself. Considering Von Clausewitz's origins for the idea is an important reference point to keep in mind. It is a powerful and transformational means, rather than the objective.

2. Identify the key areas that are within your control that may be important in achieving your goal

This may be a long list and is very specific to your situation. I list some examples below for various types of organisations. In no case is it intended to be an exhaustive list.

A typical business:
- Product quality
- Customer retention
- Customer service
- New product innovation
- Customer acquisition
- Pricing
- Culture
- Staff turn-over and/or engagement scores

A school:
- Position on exam performance league tables
- Quality and/or quantity of university places gained by students
- Attendance records
- Staff turnover
- External evaluation scores

A sports team:
- Goals scored
- Goals conceded
- Ball possession percentage
- Pass completion percentage

Though these are examples only, there are a few important points to draw out.

First, it is important not simply to identify the key areas that lie within your control, but to make an honest assessment of your team's current performance in each area. You should know this from your baseline. Which areas, if any, are you good or great at presently? Therefore, do you decide to focus on areas of relative strength or relative weakness?

Second, few teams or organisations can do only one of these and totally ignore the others. There's no point scoring more goals per game but conceding even more.

The aim of your *Schwerpunkt* is to achieve *relative* improvement of performance when measured against your other KPIs.

3. Choosing your *schwerpunkt*

There are two primary drivers in deciding upon your *schwerpunkt,* and we have so far in this chapter considered both.

The first is to consider it as an entirely internal decision, made without direct consideration of an individual competitor. In oversupplied markets, where there are many organisations competing on roughly equal terms, this is likely to be your best approach. For example, if you are an mid-table football team, there is little point deciding your *schwerpunkt* based on the relative weakness of a single competitor – what about the other eighteen in the league?

This is the case in my own industry, marketing services. Every business within the sector is essentially identical in its make-up and ambition (much as they like to claim otherwise). And it is enormously oversupplied. There are, however, businesses within it that significantly outperform (or underperform) others. For those who pay attention, there are clear areas where a dramatic relative improvement of performance pays disproportionate dividends.

We have already met Pixar, and will study them in a little more detail in Chapter 7. Their ambition was to be a hugely successful film-maker and consequently a hugely successful business. Their *schwerpunkt* is their culture. The entirety of Catmull's book describes their relentless striving to refine their culture, freeing it of the constraints of hierarchy and enabling it to attract the very best and brightest. This is a wholly inward-focused *schwerpunkt*, one where they set their own standards, and the metrics are primarily relative to internal performance. It is also one of great and enduring success.

Tesla and Sensodyne, on the other hand, in markets with relatively high barriers to entry, chose weak points in their competitor's line. The actions they took were internal, but the focus was at least partly driven by the external conditions (and opportunities) they saw.

4. Focus

If your overall objective provides direction, *Schwerpunkt* provides the means.

Your *schwerpunkt* is the cornerstone of your strategy. You must communicate clearly and frequently what you have chosen and why. You must then orient yourselves around two questions:

    i. What does it take to execute it brilliantly?
   ii. What can we let go of?

5. What does it take to be brilliant?

There is an implicit understanding in Von Clausewitz's work, that for a *Schwerpunkt* to be successful, it must be executed well. There are, of course, many examples of them failing. Wellington prevailed at Waterloo not through the genius of his attack (he certainly had no *schwerpunkt*) but rather through his ability to negate that of Napoleon. It was enough in this instance for Wellington not to lose; his opponent had to win. Much is the same for many market-leading businesses. They don't always have to win, they just have to not lose (and therefore maintain their dominant position).

Schwerpunkt only works if it is done well, with full-fat, full-blooded ambition. The key questions you must now ask are what does it mean to do it brilliantly and how are you going to do that. As we've established, that requires you and your teams to make choices around not only where you will focus your efforts, but where you will not.

Tesla's success is not simply a result of being an electric

car company, rather, their most important early investor, Elon Musk, challenged them to launch a revolutionary electric car. Prior to Tesla, electric cars had been seen much like low-alcohol beer: better for you (and the environment) but not a patch on the original. Musk turned that concept on its head. Tesla succeeded because they chose a ground where their competitors found it hard to fight *and* they executed the idea brilliantly.

Your ambition should be not simply improvement but, at this one thing, to be the best. If you fall short, and are only second or third best, then for most organisations, most of the time, that would be an immeasurable improvement. Aim for better and you'll hardly move.

6. What can you let go of?

Point 6, and we finally get to the nub.

My CEO client may well have done a reasonable job at most of the above. But what she really wanted to know was how could she ever hope to achieve meaningful long-term change when the urgent demands of the present seemed so unrelenting.

It is the central question for change leaders: how to achieve greater results with an essentially unchanged resource pool.

The answer is not to keep driving yourself harder and harder (this, for obvious reasons, is a bad idea) or vainly dream of more resources, but rather to redistribute the resources you have more effectively. (In this context, resources are always some combination of time, people and money.) If, on your graphic equaliser, one slider goes up, another, somewhere, must go down. If you don't acknowledge this fact, then you won't move forward.

You therefore have to decide how to redeploy and refocus the resources at your disposal: maintaining the status quo in some areas, affording you the time, space and energy to foment revolution in your one most important other. These are choices only you can make, but make them you must.

This is why focus, communication and alignment are so important. Unless everyone is clear on the *schwerpunkt*, they (and you) will continue to be dragged to and fro by the demands of the everyday. You must make and collectively buy in to a single simple statement of intent. For example:

> *The thing that matters most to us, above everything else,*
> *and the surest way to get us to number one, is to have*
> *the best customer service.*

This doesn't mean other demands on time and resources are unimportant; they are just clearly agreed to be less important than this. Resource allocation can be made accordingly.

7. Be remorseless, determined, and settle in for the long haul

Tides and currents will attempt to pull you from your course. Fires will break out that must be extinguished. Stakeholders will poke their noses in and ask annoying questions. But to succeed you have to be thick-skinned, clear-headed, determined and settle in for the long haul. Being great at anything doesn't happen overnight, though with the right level of determination and effort you'll be surprised how quickly you can progress.

It may even be that you decide you have made a wrong call. Even this isn't entirely bad news; change your mind. And if, in the intervening period, you have focused hard and made good progress in one important area, it is hardly wasted effort.

Just don't do it too often. Not many organisations are truly best-in-class at anything, so if yours comes close in one important area you're doing a lot of things right.

Postscript

If you execute well you will propel your team or organisation forward. If you run a sports team and your proportion of goals scored to goals conceded increases, you will, without doubt, improve your league position. Does it guarantee you will win the league? Of course not. Not least because a competitor may outperform you.

You will, however, have delivered dramatic and visible change that moved you significantly closer to your ultimate objective, change that has fundamentally improved the landscape of your organisation, meaning subsequent actions can be taken against an already altered (and improved) backdrop.

In Chapter 8, we consider change as a loop, a contingent process that does not happen in isolation. Sensodyne carved out a huge global market for themselves, but their success means that they too are now being disrupted and so must respond. And Colgate didn't sit still; they are, after all, still number one.

NO BULLSH*T *SCHWERPUNKT*

How do you decide where to begin? Attempting to do everything results in achieving nothing. Focusing on the point of maximum effect (the *schwerpunkt*) is how you break free and move rapidly towards your goal.

Change everything: change nothing

- The temptation for change leaders is simply to throw themselves into trying to fix everything. The problem is, this doesn't work.
- The dual pressures of constrained resources and heightened expectations make *Schwerpunkt* critical to your success.

Implementation

- Create a clear, bold and ambitious objective.
- *Schwerpunkt* is a powerful and transformational means, rather than the end.
- Identify the key areas within your control.
- The aim of your *schwerpunkt* is to achieve a *relative* improvement of performance when measured against your other KPIs.
- Decide on your point of maximum pressure.
- Communicate your reasons, ambitions and actions widely.
- What does it take to execute it brilliantly?
- Identify what you can let go of (at least for now).
- Be remorseless.

7

CULTURE

You must understand what culture is, what you need yours to be
and how you can change it. An effective organisational culture
enables people to achieve things for themselves, for others and
for the team that would not otherwise have been possible.

Ultimately, beyond all these abstractions of strategy, of organisation, of processes. At the end the issue is, how do we change the context ... How do we create Fontainebleau Forest inside [our] companies.
Professor Sumantra Ghoshal

The single biggest factor behind the resurgence was that [the captain] played the way he asked the team to play. He has never waivered [sic] from that, even when he hasn't been scoring ...
The Times

Fontainebleau in springtime

On film, the late Professor Sumantra Ghoshal appears a slight figure, but with room-filling charisma. Even through the filter of grainy, low-res video, his eyes sparkle with a mischievous energy. A native of Kolkata, Ghoshal served, amongst other roles, at INSEAD, as Professor of Strategic and International Management at London Business School, and was the founding Dean of the Indian School of Business in Hyderabad.

An expert on organisational culture, he argued that, despite the best efforts of leaders and development programmes, people don't fundamentally change. Context, he believed, was everything. Speaking at the World Economic Forum, he illustrated his argument with a simple parable.

Every year, he told his audience, he would return to visit his native city in the month of July, the timing dictated by his children's school holidays. 'Now Calcutta is a wonderful town in winter, autumn and spring,' he begins, 'but summer? Well. The temperature is 102 to 103, the humidity is about 99 per cent, and [when I visit] I feel very tired. Most of my vacation I'm tired, I'm indoors.'

By contrast, he continues, 'I used to live in Fontainebleau, and this I genuinely challenge you. Go to the forest of Fontainebleau in spring; go with a firm desire to have a leisurely walk. And you can't. The moment you enter the forest there is something about the crispness of the air, there is something about the smell of the trees in spring: you want to run, you want to jog, you want to catch a branch, do something.'

This, he argued, was comparable to the environment inside so many of the organisations he studied. 'Most companies ... have created downtown Calcutta in summer ... then complain [that the employees] are lazy, [they] don't take initiative, [they] don't take cooperation ... Ultimately, beyond all these abstractions of strategy, of organisation, of processes; at the end the issue is, how do we change the context? How,' he concluded, 'do we create Fontainebleau Forest inside companies?'

It's a beautifully simple thought experiment. As you listen, you can smell the damp moss, the high notes of pine and low of wild garlic, feel the warmth and chill between the dappled patches of sunlight. Even his brief description is invigorating.

There's an eight-minute video online of the full speech. It's easy to find. My most honest advice is to put this book down, find it and watch it. I have only one caveat. In the version I found, somebody had thoughtfully laid his words over a stock montage featuring smiley, plastic people high-fiving accompanied by a soundtrack from an insurance commercial. All of which invoked a smell more redolent of manure than Big Sur after rain. So perhaps switch the screen off and simply listen to his words.

For Ghoshal, culture is the red thread that links high corporate strategy, 'with me, the salesman in Lyon' – his putative distant, but hard-working employee on the receiving end of head office's missives and mired in their dysfunctional culture. Companies, he argues, have a smell, one you can distinguish immediately on entering. What does that smell tell you of the place? Too often, strategy, rather than liberating, simply becomes a box to constrain, the dimensions of which become smaller and smaller the further down the organisational hierarchy you go.

'Companies create this elaborate infrastructure of systems; planning systems, budgeting systems, financial systems, all of it boils down, by the time it travels down to me [the hypothetical salesperson in Lyon], the smell it creates for me, is compliance, control. It exists to control me.'

Resistant to change or unable to change?

Constraint, compliance, control and contract, he argues, are all too often the smell that 'management' creates. In this world, leaders complain that their people lack energy and initiative, that they don't cooperate. They blame the company's struggles on their workforce rather than looking to themselves. However, it is they, through the cultural context they create (the smell, to use Ghoshal's language) who are the real constraint. People's behaviours, he argues, are entirely contextual. Management complain that their people are resistant to change, yet where and how, he wonders, are they going to find the new behaviours change demands if they remain trapped in their ever-shrinking boxes?

Does this sound familiar? For many, it will. And if it doesn't, beware that it isn't simply because you are not the salesperson in Lyon, but the person at the top, blissfully unaware, or unwilling to accept, that their behaviours are Ghoshal's four Cs: **constraint**, **compliance**, **control** and **contract**.

All change is culture change

It is impossible to undertake a change programme without also considering culture. All change resolves to people's behaviours: individuals doing things differently, interacting differently, behaving differently to how they had before. If culture is the sum of individual behaviours, then all organisational change is in large part concerned with changing the culture.

Of course, there will always be many other (often significant) aspects to consider: the integration of an acquisition, the development of a new capability or product, the revision of long-established systems, processes and structures. However, in practice it is impossible to disentangle these from an accompanying cultural change. Even if the culture you begin with is broadly one you believe to be healthy and well-suited to its task, you should ensure you are taking nothing about it for granted and that you understand it well.

In circumstances where you feel the culture is either poorly understood or more Kolkata in July than Fontainebleau in April, you could (perhaps should) consider it to be at the heart of your change programme. If your culture is weak, then your organisation will not become strong without changing it. It's as simple as that. There may be other things you wish to do, but you cannot be strong without a strong culture. If you consider your culture to be already strong, then you need to understand it and carefully sustain it.

Ghoshal's ideal culture

There were, though, some companies Ghoshal met who he said smelt different, who smelt like we imagine the forest might. In these companies he found the defining behaviours are not control and constraint, but **stretch, discipline, trust** and **support**.

I don't share these as the only answers; you must find your own understanding of what a great culture means to you. Nevertheless, whatever you decide, it will be defined by behaviours, not words.

- **Stretch**

We refer here not to stretch in the sense of financial scale, but to stretch as an ambition, where every employee is trying to achieve more rather than less. These are the people we met in the Thrive quadrant in Chapter 5.

- **Discipline**

Rather than control and compliance, collective respect and alignment. Decisions, once taken, are embraced, rather than being undone in the corridor immediately when the dissenters leave the room; if a meeting is due to start at 9 a.m., everybody is there, ready to go at 9 a.m.

Here, discipline manifests as mutual respect.

- **Support**

The opposite of control. The role of leaders, throughout the organisation is to help their teams win, through access to resources, coaching and effective guidance.

- **Trust**

The opposite of contract. You may be my closest colleague in the organisation, or you may be on the other side of the world, but if you carry the same card that's good enough for me.

These should not be confused with corporate values. They are not how the organisations describe themselves, but rather are Ghoshal's own descriptions of common behaviours he finds where effective cultures enhance rather than constrain individual, and therefore collective, performance. Furthermore, he concludes by urging us not to intellectualise or get hung up on his four words, but rather to imagine the smell that can be created in your organisation if those were the norms of behaviour.

Imagine if your organisation smelt like Fontainebleau in springtime.

Culture is the environment a leader creates in order for their team to outperform

Though all organisations have a culture, many are blissfully unaware what theirs actually is. Some think they know, but are wrong; a great many are in denial and convince themselves that the culture is whatever is described in the annual report or on the website. Others have a vague sense of what they would like it to be, but little idea about how to get there.

It is therefore no surprise that, at all levels, it is possible to find great cynicism when the subject of culture arises. Not because people don't think it matters, but because cynicism exists in the gap between what is said and what is done. And when it comes to culture, in many organisations this gap is very large indeed.

The best way to understand what shapes real culture is through behaviours rather than values. Values might matter as a statement of corporate intent, but often do little to directly shape a culture, mostly because they are difficult for people to translate into their working lives, other than in a very general sense. Effective culture is shaped by, understood through and primarily concerned with influencing the behaviours of the individuals in your team(s).

Pixar: a culture of relentless self-improvement

Pixar are today one of the best-known and most admired companies on the planet, co-founded by Steve Jobs, presumably when he had a little time over lunch in between transforming the computer market, the communications market and the music industry. Their first feature film, *Toy Story*, was the first to be produced entirely by computer animation, and their name is now a byword for quality and creativity. In his book *Creativity, Inc.*, Jobs's co-founder Ed Catmull describes the secrets of their enduring success.

Creativity, Inc. is a book entirely about the commercial power of an effective culture. What is striking is the seriousness and effort the company took over a long period of time to understand and continually develop their culture, carefully and thoughtfully analysing their own successes and failures to refine how they worked, improve the relationships between their employees, explore how the hierarchy helped or hindered their progress and more.

Their ambition was lofty (which comes as no surprise

with Jobs and the helm) and culture-driven. Catmull is explicit about both the liberating and (at times) the constricting effects of their culture, and the book's primary theme is the continuous efforts they made to accentuate its positive and address its negative effects on their product.

'We were blessed with a remarkable group of employees who valued change, risk and the unknown ... How,' he asks, 'could we enable the talents of these people, keep them happy, and not let the inevitable complexities that come with any collaborative endeavour undo us?'

The following passage is about creativity, but has almost universal application.

> People tend to think of creativity as a mysterious solo act ... [but] creativity involves a large number of people from different disciplines working together effectively to solve a great many problems ... what's tough is getting talented people to work effectively with one another. That takes trust and respect which we as managers can't mandate; it must be earned over time. What we can do is construct an environment that nurtures everyone's creativity.

Pixar determined to do this through identifying three clear behaviours. What is interesting is the prominent role communication, candour and change play in how they describe their most important cultural objectives:

1. Everyone must have the freedom to communicate with anyone.
2. It must be safe for everyone to offer ideas.
3. Change is a continuous process.

Through their journey from tiny start-up to global powerhouse, they came to understand that talent is a construct that exists within a cultural context, and that neither can be understood without the other. Their endeavour to maintain a high-performing creative culture is their version of Professor Ghoshal's stroll through Fontainebleau Forest. What *Creative, Inc.* leaves the reader with, however, is not only the power of such a culture, but the determination, single-mindedness, effort and collective honesty it takes to get there.

The performance equation

Culture change – indeed arguably all change – has at its heart the ambition to improve the performance of groups of individuals against a defined objective. Team performance can be understood as the product of two variables, both of which are largely, if not wholly, within your control: the cultural environment and the sum of talent in the team. It can be expressed as shown below:

team performance = talent x culture

In leading change it is likely, if not certain, that you will seek to change at least one, if not both, of these variables at different points. We have already seen how, in their different ways, Ghoshal and Catmull understood the centrality of this equation to organisational performance, and that, for both, culture is the dominating factor.

Over many years I have come to the belief that we need to ask ourselves three questions in order to optimise our teams. The first two are as follows:

1. Are people working in an environment that allows them to perform at their best?
2. Are they clear what their personal objectives are?

Only after we have answered these can we ask:

3. Are they good enough and/or the right person for the role?

Questions 1 and 2 should dominate all considerations when evaluating individual performance.

It is for this reason that a person moving from team A to team B might find that their happiness, satisfaction and performance changes dramatically. They move from a hero to a zero, or vice versa. We've all seen it, maybe even experienced it. It's not the individual who has changed, but the context. As Ghoshal observed, some leaders complain that their people aren't team players, that 'they don't get it', that they're slow, impulsive, or careless; they blame the workforce rather than looking to themselves.

I have come to believe that, in an organisational or team context, the idea of an absolute measure of somebody's ability is all but impossible to obtain. For any of us, there is only contextual performance: how well an individual is able to perform given the environment they find themselves in.

We see this everywhere and intuitively take it for granted, yet when it comes to our own teams we seem so often to forget. This morning, sipping tea, I came across the following headline: 'Erik ten Hag: Happiness is key to Marcus Rashford's revival', in reference to the Manchester United manager's comments on their faltering striker. What else is that, but a comment on their culture?

Are penalty shoot-outs a lottery?

In 2022, Liverpool beat Chelsea in a penalty shoot-out in the FA Cup final, the oldest football competition in the world. Truth be told, it was, as they say, a game for the purists, 0–0 after 120 minutes of play. As always, the penalty shoot-out seemed an unsatisfactory way to settle the contest, containing none of the essential elements that make the beautiful game just that, trading elegance and skill for drama and a guaranteed conclusion. It's a lottery, isn't it, goes the eternal debate.

Several days after the final, an article written by Professor Geir Jordet of the Norwegian School of Sport Sciences took my eye. Jordet lauded the winning manager Jürgen Klopp and criticised the loser, Thomas Tuchel. He argued that, far from being a lottery, culture, as personified by the manager, could make all the difference.

'A penalty shoot-out is a psychological game starting with how the manager communicates,' he began. Klopp,

Jordet claimed, told his players who amongst them would be stepping up within sixty seconds of the full-time whistle, and he did it individually, conducting private conversations with each rather than in the adrenaline-fuelled chaos of a post-match huddle. 'The process [was] intimate, safe and loving,' he observed.

According to Jordet, Klopp had completed this within two minutes, while his opponent was still deciding his takers. Tuchel, having finally drawn up his list, told his team collectively from the middle of a mass huddle – a common mistake in such situations Jordet believes. 'What could have been a smooth and final reminder to the team becomes erratic, rushed and stressed.' In addition, Tuchel then discussed their individual tactics in front of their teammates, increasing the pressure further.

'Liverpool were 1–0 up before the shoot-out had even begun,' Jordet concluded.

Post-rationalised? Possibly. Impossible to prove? Certainly. However, if after 120 minutes of football the two teams find themselves tied, then where might they find the edge to complete from the spot what they could not conclude in open play?

The shoot-out is an interesting petri dish. For professional footballers, it is hardly a measure of skill, rather a measure of nerve and the ability to perform those skills under extreme pressure. Such is the relative simplicity of the functional aspect of the task, it effectively rules out ability as a differentiator and shifts it to a battle of will and nerve. If performance is the product of talent and culture, then it is reasonable to conclude that the ability to create a more effective (in this case, scoring more penalties) culture will be the deciding factor. Which, Professor Jordet argues, is exactly what Jürgen Klopp did. Culture may appear to be soft, squishy and intangible; however, its effects can be anything but.

Optimising team performance

I recently took up golf. For someone who has played tennis since they were nine, the idea of hitting a ball that just lay there waiting to be struck was an enticing prospect. It transpired, however, that the sullen, alluring, static ball was the very essence of the game's fiendishness. Technology has, of course, got a gadget for that. These days, every coach worth their salt uses a TrackMan (other equally expensive brands are available). Possessing the same Doppler shift radar systems as fifth-generation fighter aircraft, it tracks around forty different aspects of your swing and ball contact, all of which confirming what you already knew – that you'd shanked it into the gorse.

A key data point it provides is how close you were to hitting *your* optimum shot, measured against the machine's baseline assessment of your ability. Relative to your current skill level, did you over- or under-optimise?

It is possible to consider how teams work in a similar way. They have a collective maximum potential, the sum of the abilities of those in the team. But how often do those individuals reach their personal best, never mind the team over-optimising? I have regular conversations with leaders of teams big and small, and an inevitable topic will be a gripe about some member or other, sometimes a passing frustration, sometimes something of far greater significance – many not dissimilar to those Professor Ghoshal encountered.

A common complaint relates to a person's specific skills, attitude or work ethic: 'They just need to learn to be better at ...' But conversations such as these nearly always miss the point. A person's performance is a function of their baseline skills and the environment they find themselves in. Indeed, it is one of the reasons, I believe, that traditional performance reviews achieve very little, or at least are misused and misunderstood. The issue is not whether your team's skills can be developed. Of course they can. The more pressing strategic issue for you as the change leader is whether you have managed to optimise the performance of your team as a whole. In many cases where I see teams underperform, the issue is diagnosed by the leader as a skills deficit or poor attitude; in reality, the team's optimum state is easily good enough to achieve all that is asked of them. So why don't they reach it?

Imagine your team as those 1980s Top Trumps cards. A bit crass? Of course. But we do it all the time; we often evaluate people against a set of semi-scientific measures. Look at your team right now. Score them, just a simple measure – out of five, perhaps? You need to strip out your emotions, your own baggage (as best you can). Consider them at their very best rather than their most irritating, perhaps the hopes you had the day you hired them. The day you had a row with them in the morning and then saw them absolutely smash a client presentation in the afternoon. Consider this their individual optimum.

What's your team's optimum?

In a team of five, sketch it out on the back of an envelope like this:

William: 3.5
Megan: 4
Harry: 3
Fergie: 4.5
Kate: 4
Total: 19/25 (76 per cent)

So your team's optimum score is 76 per cent. That's an A/B. That's pretty, good right? If you perform at that level, you're going to win way more than you lose.

Of course, you could do better. You could switch out Harry. You could coach and cajole William. You could train them to raise their baseline performance. All of which is sensible and professional. I know you're also saying to yourself, 'Yes, but this isn't real! Fergie might be a 4.5 at her best, but most of the time she's a 2. She drives me mad. She's always moaning about wanting to be promoted and complaining behind our backs.' But you've beaten me to it. Just like the golf ball that I hit sweetly out of the middle of the club but hooked yards to the left, your team is way under-optimised.

Now score your team as a collective. How are you doing? You need to be honest. There's no risk, there's only you here. A-, B+, C? Worse?

The difference between your optimal and your reality is the extent to which, like my golf swing, your team is under-optimised. A team that has a theoretical max of 76 per cent, however unscientifically measured, is good enough. Good enough to win most pitches, crack most problems, perform alongside the best in class. But if the real-world performance of that team is a C, then you're way off the pace.

Few leaders find themselves blessed with a team of stellar talents. Yet great leaders lead teams that consistently outperform. Their people seem more satisfied and more productive; they get promoted and go on to have better careers. This is because great leaders don't obsess about the nuance of the skill sets of the individuals. They do matter; it's just that, from a team performance point of view, they matter less than the leader's ability to get the team to optimise its performance.

A culture is as strong as its weakest point

A strong culture enables organisations to withstand significant shocks, but every culture is vulnerable to those within it who are unwilling to buy in to the behaviours that it demands. These people are not mavericks; a strong culture has room for them and many other types. Rather, they are individuals who, rather like NoNo, do not buy in to your vision of why culture is so important and the role all (including them) must play in its maintenance. Culture isn't something for the little people, or for everyone else, it's for all. Or else it is severely diminished. The more senior these people, the bigger the problem – as always. Individuals such as these who have no interest in fitting within the culture will ultimately not just damage team performance, but fundamentally undermine the work you have done to date.

So important are these people that sometimes their simple removal is sufficient to catalyse change. Jack Welch was an iconic but polarising leader, so much so that my previous book received several one-star reviews simply for mentioning him. Nevertheless, one of his ideas is so useful in understanding the power of culture that it's impossible not to revisit it. So here goes again.

Welch was the CEO of General Electric when it was the largest company in the world. He demanded very high levels of performance from his businesses, and was uncompromising in his expectations. However, he was no simplistic cost-cutter. He understood, and ensured that his leaders understood, the importance of culture to their success, and how this should be maintained. Or could be undermined.

		NO	YES
DELIVERS RESULTS	YES	CHANGE HAPPENS WHEN THESE PEOPLE GO	SKY'S THE LIMIT
	NO	FIRE	COACH
		NO	YES
			GETS US

Welch's grid, shown above, is mostly self-explanatory, but it carries a single very powerful message. Underperforming units, he claimed, only began to change when they removed people in the top-left box, those who delivered results, but did not fit with the culture. He put cultural consistency ahead of short-term profit, in the belief that by staying true to the culture, and demonstrating so through their behaviours, they would ultimately be a higher-performing business. It's another of those slides that when I share it people sit up and pay attention. Not least because we can all think of examples of our own.

It's a powerful example of how cultural change works and a recognition that any culture is only as strong as its weakest point. If you tolerate those who refuse to stay true to the culture then the cynicism grows and you yourself are judged to have fallen short of the behaviours you have said are important. If you act, your culture changes. Words alone, when it comes to culture, are cheap in the short term, but expensive in the long.

It is a perfect, simple and everyday example of culture being the behaviour of leadership and how leaders can quickly and easily drive cultural change. Just this act, simple, yet often difficult to do, can transform. Indeed, Welch argued that transformation was impossible without it.

We've all faced situations such as this. We have all heard the reasons why such a step would be impossible. But at least some among us will recall the liberation, freedom and the fresh scents of moss and pine when at last such action was taken. This is how and why cultural change can be achieved a lot more quickly than many believe.

Culture starts (and ends) with you

The easiest way to understand the culture of an organisation is to realise that it is an expression of the behaviour of the leaders. In the examples given earlier, the cultures of the two football clubs are expressed via the behaviour of their managers; Welch, by publishing his grid, insisted that culture came first. In many situations, it is something we instinctively accept, yet often leaders do little to consciously understand or shape their own behaviours in ways that will positively influence the culture and, by direct implication, their own success.

Changing culture is both as simple and difficult as that, but there is no change you can make that will have an impact as great or as enduring.

I am, however, aware that an injunction to simply behave differently may sound daunting. But what I have attempted to show, through Ghoshal's forest stroll, Catmull's relentless focus and Welch's determination to walk the walk, is that it need not be as difficult as it sounds. The requirement is not for you, or those around you, to be different people. That is not just unrealistic, it is mostly not possible. Rather, it is about being clear about the culture you need in order to succeed, and working out how you will establish some fundamental principles that everyone, should they set their minds to it, can employ. Starting, of course, with you.

The five universal features of great cultures

What I have come to believe, and what is interesting about Ghoshal and Catmull's examples, is that, despite their contrasting language – Catmull that of a West Coast start-up, Ghoshal of a business school professor – many of the features of a successful culture are universal. Not just that, but these are things we can all do, indeed, they are things we all like to think we already do (even though, with a little self-reflection we will certainly recognise room for improvement). The problem is, left to our own devices, we also do lots of other things as well. We need to understand which behaviours are most important in sustaining a high performance culture and set about working out how to be the personal embodiment of them.

I believe all great cultures have these behaviours at their heart: language may vary, the mix and manifestation may vary, but these traits are there in all. And anyone can do them should they choose to. I don't present this as the only solution, but I do know that any leader who follows these five principles will build a very effective and high-performing culture.

1. Great cultures don't just happen

All great and enduring cultures must exist at the front, not the back, of the leader's mind. And arguably that of everybody in the organisation.

In too many organisations, understanding of culture is vague and ill-formed. Simply by bringing it into the light, stating what you believe and that it matters, will create change. It must remain high on your to-do list; neglected, it will shrivel, but with regular attention it will grow, strengthen and adapt as you do.

Great cultures are a restless hive mind, always hunting ways to build their strengths, plug their gaps and fix their flaws.

2. High trust

Trust requires everyone to feel they are part of the same team, with the same objective and being judged by the same criteria. Most organisations are full of ambitious, bright people who want to do well, yet the 'smell' slowly squeezes the life from them.

Trust, we're told, must be earned, but if you're the leader and you want change, trust is a choice. This doesn't mean trusting person A over person B; rather it is a behaviour that you do or don't choose to exhibit. A culture that lacks trust ultimately is a culture that constrains performance through the imposition of unnecessary structure, process and bureaucracy. Chop these away and trust must fill the gap.

Ultimately, if you don't trust the people you have, don't simply impose a set of limiting and constraining structures and behaviours. Instead, get people you do trust. But then get out of their way and enable them to thrive.

3. Safety and support

A strong culture feels safe and supportive; it feels as though it's got your back. Leaders, rather than con-straining, strive for ways to help their teams and the individuals within them grow, to be great for their careers.

Everyone is clear on their objectives and clear on the behaviours that the organisation says it values, which must include respecting each other, effective conflict management, mutual support and the importance of being a great team member, no matter what your job title.

If a great culture enables people to achieve things they otherwise wouldn't, it is a prerequisite that they are able to say things, do things, try things and, from time to time, make errors they otherwise wouldn't. In the wrong culture these actions are too risky for people to take, and they shrink, the performance of the whole diminished.

Average cultures value not losing over winning. Great cultures value winning over not losing. Change leaders are here to win, and to do so you need an environment where the fear of 'getting it wrong' doesn't get in the way.

4. Great communication

Communicating well is how people remain connected to each other, understand each other, have a clear understanding of their individual role, the collective ambition and the progress that is being made. It is also how conflicts are resolved, problems solved and great ideas come to the fore. Organisations need hierarchy, but the best leaders don't allow it to get in the way of effective communication, either upwards or down.

Without a determination to encourage and enable great, clear and honest communication throughout the organisation, many people, especially those outside its highest ranks, will be constrained and limited in their ability to fully contribute and achieve their full potential.

5. Consistency and predictability

Cultures must be consistent. Their behaviours apply to everybody, all the time.

We are all human. This doesn't mean people never say things, do things or behave in a way that is counter to the culture – they will, and it's normal. However, these need to be recognised as such. This is why effective communication matters.

The behaviours must apply to all, and the more senior you are the more responsibility you have to walk the walk. We all makes mistakes; in fact, in great cultures these are accepted as an important part of future success. However, those who consistently refuse to embrace the culture must go. Great cultures can be very powerful, but they are only as strong as their weakest point.

Organisations have many different ways to describe their culture. As we've established, many more hardly bother at all. I think there are compelling reasons to use language specific to your situation; it can make your messaging easier to remember, help internal branding and aid connection with your stakeholders. However, it certainly doesn't have to be unique to be successful. As always, the ultimate key to success is not in the snazzy words but the quality of execution.

Becoming the culture

As a leader, of a team big or small, you must be the physical embodiment of the change you want to create. These days I often work in our communal café rather than at my desk. It is surprising how many people stop by to talk, raise questions or make suggestions. It's one way I cut through the layers of hierarchy, something we have returned to throughout this book. These connections really matter, as Deverell, Ghoshal and Catmull all recognised. It doesn't on its own define the culture, but it does play a role, and is a conscious and deliberate choice.

It is rather unfashionable to say it in a world of 'authentic' leaders, but leadership is a performance, one determined by the culture you aim to build. Your actions will always speak stronger than your words; therefore, if you've had a row with your partner that morning and need to give an inspiring talk to your team before they meet a new client, you simply have to shake it off; if you lose a major bid, you cannot sit with your head down on the desk. At least not for very long.

- You can be disappointed, but not despairing.
- You can be angry, but not capricious or spiteful.
- You can be economic with the truth, but not lie.

- You can not know the answer, but not appear lost.
- You can celebrate, but must be inclusive.
- You can be close to some, but not exclude others.

If you set yourself these personal markers then the culture will follow. It's not all you must do, but by being the change you want to see you will be well on your way.

A five-step programme for cultural change

In talking to leaders about culture I often encounter a kind of fatalism: a belief that though it may be critical to how a team or organisation functions, it is all but impossible to change.

This is a classic misunderstanding (or excuse, take your pick). Culture is simply an aggregation of individual behaviours; change the behaviours, change the culture. Potentially difficult? Yes. A long, drawn-out process? Not necessarily.

There is, however, little point in doing all the sensible business-schooly stuff associated with change management if you don't consider the culture you need in order to succeed, have a clear view of how that differs from what exists currently and have a plan for how to get there.

As with all change, cultural change has three stages:

- Understand the start.
- Know where you want to get to (initially an approximation will do).

- Undertake decisive and focused action to instil change.

1. Understanding today

You must have a clear-eyed understanding of what the culture is today. This is possibly the most important and significant piece of work you can undertake as a leader of change. **Most organisations and team leaders are not able to answer this question.**

Action: Dedicate time, resource and energy to get an impartial read on the real culture in your team. Understand specifically the ways in which it works well and ways in which it hinders performance. Use the principles outlined in the previous sections as markers. As with any baseline, understanding is the prelude to solving.

2. A cultural ambition

Values are almost entirely useless when attempting to understand or define culture. Culture is shaped by and expressed through how people behave.

Action: Write out longhand the kind of environment you would like to create. It should be a straightforward, easy-to-understand ambition – your version of Fontainebleau in spring. Use Ghoshal's and Catmull's examples to identify the markers that will define your progress.

3. Consult, communicate, let go

Communicate, communicate, communicate. Culture must be understood and owned by all. It is a living, breathing entity, not a fixed point. Just the act of focusing on it will begin to evolve and improve it.

Action: Be explicit about why culture matters and publish your recommendations.

Take feedback. Let go. Allow the culture to evolve beyond your full control. Publish what you believe and what you learn.

Keep it simple, actionable and clear. Avoid jargon and management speak. Be humble and acknowledge where you are today and areas where the change may be most difficult.

4. Moments and totems

What are the most important moments when your culture manifests? Evaluate how these must change as the culture changes. Make totems of new ones.

Action: Identify key moments that will signify the culture you want. These could include many of the areas we have discussed so far. Just a few examples:

- The internal environment
- Where people sit and how the space is used
- A review of processes and structures – what will need to change?
- Culture-focused training (for example, conflict resolution)
- How performance reviews are run
- How key meetings are organised and run
- Social events
- How new joiners are inducted
- The focus of your website and internal communications
- KPIs

You must introduce opportunities for new behaviours to be seen and to impact, as well as signifying intent and change through action.

5. Perpetual motion
Culture is a living, breathing thing.

The surest way to embed cultural change and, ultimately, the culture you want is to make it part of your business strategy. By publicly focusing on it and leading an ongoing conversation around it you will ensure it changes for the better. Most cultures are felt, but forgotten. Make sure yours is understood and owned by all. It will necessarily be in permanent evolution, but an ongoing dialogue about what it is, what you'd like it to be and the varying ways it helps and hinders the delivery of the results you need is the best way to mould it into the powerful force for change that you need. Whatever else you decide, openness and honesty are the surest way to build a great culture.

Action: The term the Observer Effect means that the act of observing will influence the phenomenon being observed. Nowhere is this more true than with organisational culture.

- Understand that the culture will be a permanent work-in-progress. Expect to not have all the answers and that it will develop in unexpected ways, some good, some bad. Left untended, beware: it will evolve in ways you may not like.

- Name it, describe it, discuss it, share it and keep it on your to-do list.
- Invite feedback, criticism and fresh ideas.
- Listen, observe and, most importantly, learn.
- Make it a priority and keep it a priority

NO BULLSH*T CULTURE

You must understand what culture is, what you need yours to be and how you can change it. An effective organisational culture enables people to achieve things for themselves, for others and for the team that would not otherwise have been possible.

Fontainebleau in springtime: Professor Ghoshal's ideal culture

From: constraint, compliance, control and contract.

To: stretch, discipline, support and trust.

Team performance = talent x culture

Ask yourself two critical questions before evaluating individual performance:

1. Are they in an environment that enables them to perform at their best?
2. Are they clear about what their personal objectives are?

Five universal features of great cultures

1. **Great cultures don't just happen**

   They are a restless hive mind, always hunting for ways to build their strengths, plug their gaps and fix their flaws.

2. **High trust**

   Everyone feels part of the same team, working towards the same collective objective, being judged by the same criteria.

3. **Safety and support**

   Leaders, rather than constraining, strive for ways to help their teams and the individuals within them grow, to be great for their careers.

4. **Great communication**

   Without clear and honest communication, many people will be constrained and limited in their ability to fully contribute and achieve their maximum potential.

5. **Consistency and predictability**

   Cultures must be consistent. Their behaviours apply to everyone, all the time.

A five-step programme for cultural change

1. **Understand the culture today**

   Most organisations are not able to answer the question, 'What defines our culture?'

2. **A cultural ambition**

   Culture is shaped by and expressed through behaviours, not values. Write out longhand the kind of environment you would like to create.

3. **Consult, communicate and let go**

   Communicate, communicate, communicate. Be explicit about why culture matters and publish your recommendations.

4. **Moments and totems**

   What are the most important moments when your culture manifests? Evaluate how these must change as the culture changes. Make totems of new ones.

5. **Perpetual motion**

   The surest way to embed cultural change and, ultimately, the culture you want is to make it part of your business strategy. Most cultures are felt, but forgotten. Make sure yours is understood and owned by all.

OODA

Change is not a smooth, linear process. It is a series of loops
that must be completed, each requiring a fresh cycle of observation,
orientation, decision and action.
You thought you'd finished? You've only just begun.

revolution (/rɛvəˈluːʃ(ə)n/)

noun

1. *A significant change in the way people do things.*
2. *A movement in a circle or curve around a central point.*

I have not failed. I've just found 10,000 ways
that won't work.
Thomas A. Edison

IN 1953, THEN SECOND LIEUTENANT John Boyd completed an unremarkable tour of duty for the US Air Force in Korea. His tour, before being rotated home, had been short: twenty-two missions rather than the usual 100, and during which he never once fired his guns in anger. On his return, Boyd was invited to attend the US Air Force's Fighter Weapons School, where he graduated top of his class. He stayed on as an instructor and rapidly rose to head the academic section where he wrote the school's tactical manual, an instruction book for aerial fighting.

From his biography, it seems Boyd wasn't an easy man, having been variously nicknamed Genghis John (for his confrontational style), the Ghetto Colonel (for his spartan life) and the Mad Major (for his leadership). However, the moniker that best captured his subsequent legend was Forty Second Boyd.

As an air combat instructor, Boyd's party piece was to challenge all comers to an aerial combat, in which he would start from a position of disadvantage (for example, at a far lower altitude than his opponent) and defeat them in under forty seconds. It's the equivalent of a boxer offering to fight with one hand tied behind their back and win in a single round. Boyd always won. Forty seconds is less time than it took you to read the first three paragraphs of this chapter. He was a real-life Maverick, Tom Cruise's character in *Top Gun*.

Aviation history is dotted with charismatic individuals like Boyd – pilots, warriors who were somehow just that bit better than the others, and consequently lived longer and destroyed more opponents. Perhaps still the best known of these is the Red Baron, the German flying ace Baron Manfred von Richthofen, so named for his characteristic scarlet painted aircraft. The highest-scoring ace of the First World War, he remains a semi-fabled figure even today, over a hundred years later (although he is now perhaps best known as Snoopy's imaginary foe in the *Peanuts* comic strips).

What set Boyd apart is that he wondered what it was, beyond simple flying ability, that these individuals and indeed that he himself possessed that enabled them to consistently win in the ultimate zero-sum game. And could it be taught and learnt?

Boyd, by now a full colonel, was a man of rare talent,

and not simply for aerial combat. He outlined the answer to his own question in his central work, a presentation of several hundred slides entitled *Discourse on Winning and Losing*, which he also summarised in a short paper, *Destruction and Creation* (1976). I've read it so you don't have to, and understood barely a word. It's on the internet, hunt it out. His central thesis combines Gödel's incompleteness theorems, Heisenberg's uncertainty principle and the second law of thermodynamics (I'm not kidding). However, Colonel Boyd's conclusions are profound, and go well beyond the gladiatorial arena of dogfighting.

Observe, orient, decide, act

Boyd's ideas are now far better known than the man. In air combat Boyd described the process of the two flyers as a loop made up of four stages: observation, orientation, decision and action – what is now known as the OODA loop.

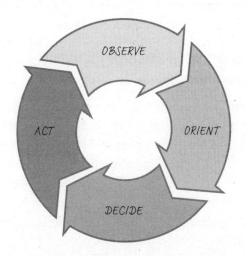

In the three-dimensional arena of the sky, the respective pilots must move along the stages of this loop in order to position their aircraft in a way that enables them to defeat their opponent; their decisions, however, are not taken in isolation but are contingent on those of their opponent. It's a kind of deadly dance; the fighters' two OODA loops intertwined. However, in simple terms, Boyd's theory is that the pilot able to get their loop inside that of their opponent – in other words, the pilot who can respond to their changing environment the fastest – wins.

OODA is not a nice snappy acronym, which in some ways is refreshing. It suggests the words have been chosen for utility and accuracy rather than as a catchy book title:

- Observe
- Orient
- Decide
- Act

You thought you'd finished?
You've only just begun

Many books on change conclude at the beginning. They tell you all the steps to get started and then stop right after the real hard work begins. I have encouraged you to start quickly, but sustainable change is neither a quick process nor, in many real-world situations, one with a clear finish line. For many leaders and organisations, the end point is more like that of a rainbow, you can see it, you can move toward it, you can cover a great distance, but you might never hold it in your hand.

There are, of course, many examples where this may seem not to be the case. Some projects have, initially, a very clearly defined end point. This is true also of Boyd's primary interest. At the end of a dogfight, the loser gets shot down.

However, even if you achieve your goal of winning the league, for example, your process cannot stop. Your opponents will have observed, oriented, decided and continued to act. They will respond to your success by altering their orientation and action to improve their chances next time you meet, in the next quarter, the next marketing campaign or the following season.

Boyd's model describes the difference between aerobatics and air fighting. The former is a solo demonstration of the pilot's pure flying ability; the latter is about winning. Consideration of the behaviour of the competition is baked into Boyd's model, which is what gives it its enduring power.

Change is not linear, but a series of loops

It is unhelpful and unrealistic to consider change as a smooth, linear process; rather, imagine it a series of loops that must be completed, each requiring a fresh cycle of observation, orientation, decision and action. Leading change in the real world is not an abstract event pursued within a closed system; it is a contingent process, executed within an open system, one characterised by unpredictability, uncertainty and even chaos. Your moves create responses that you cannot fully predict or control. Boyd advises that the faster you can complete the loops, the more likely it is that you will be able to control events and force those slower than you to respond to your actions rather than you to theirs.

In so much of what it is written and taught about change it is treated as a solo act, one that happens in isolation, like aerobatics. This is useful up to a point, but in almost any real-world context, whatever your objective: to attract better people, to win the new client, to win the league, to win more customers, to improve the department's performance, it is important, if not critical, to remember that your competition also get a vote. For each move of yours they will make their own. To prevail, you must get inside their OODA loop.

Loops of change

1. *Kaizen*

In the 1970s and 1980s, rapidly growing new economies led by Japan developed revolutionary new methods for organising and operating large organisations. Their nimble, decentralised processes, of which *Kaizen* remains the most widely known, fundamentally challenged the received post-war wisdom of how organisations could be run and, ultimately, inverted the world economic order.

Not specifically a business term, *Kaizen* is a Japanese philosophy aimed at continual improvement through all aspects of life. When applied properly, it goes beyond simple productivity improvements (how it is often characterised) and humanises the workplace. It reduces workload, eliminates unnecessary tasks and waste, and specifically aims to reduce repetitive work (and its consequent risk of errors and mistakes).

Kaizen is a neat conjunction of two of this book's most important strands:

- The process of continuous observation, orientation, decision and action (as articulated by John Boyd)
- The quest to remove hierarchical barriers in order to liberate creative problem-solving (as exemplified by Ed Catmull at Pixar)

Kaizen succeeds through bringing together the expertise of all workers to continually find better solutions to problems and spot opportunities for improvement based on the assumption that those doing a task every day best know the problems they face and how to fix them.

It is a sophisticated and powerful tool that is part process, part culture. Although wary of oversimplification, I have overlaid it onto Boyd's loop for illustrative purposes.

Observe: Begin with a careful and informed analysis of the current situation. This could be, for example, people on a production line regularly coming together to discuss how the process is working, through their assessment of recurring problems, flaws or mistakes.

Orientate: All involved make suggestions for possible improvements and changes.

Decide: The team makes a decision based on the best information available to them. *Kaizen* reduces the weight of this decision, as it implicitly recognises that this is simply a step in a process, not a one-off event.

Act: Once action is taken, both *Kaizen* and OODA regard it as simply a position on a loop. Its effects, and the actions that follow, are (re-)observed, and the process repeats.

2. Winning ugly

Brad Gilbert was a top-ten tennis player in the late 1980s and early 1990s. In his bestselling book, *Winning Ugly*, he makes a virtue out of his ability to maximise his abilities and defeat many of the more naturally talented players of his era. The book is not about the technical aspects of the game, such as how to hit a forehand or serve; rather it is concerned entirely with how to play the game to win.

Most sport is contingent, the players responding to each other's moves (an obvious exception being golf). Gilbert's book has two recurring questions:

- Do you understand what your opponent is trying to do to you?
- Are you clear what you are trying to do to them?

This is a classic example of an OODA loop. Each player should have an initial plan for victory based upon an assessment of their own relative strengths and weaknesses. However, this will inevitably run up against their opponent's strategy, the two interweaving as the game develops.

Rather than simply blunder on, as many players do, Gilbert encourages the reader to think about the circumstance they find themselves in as the game plays out – obvious, but surprisingly difficult to do. In sport and life we become consumed with our own performance, rather than understanding it as being only half of the story. Though he does not use Boyd's language, the commonalities are clear:

Observe: How is the match progressing? Are you winning or losing? How do you feel? (Emotion is a key driver of performance in sport.)

Orientate: What is your opponent doing that is working? What are they doing that is not? Similarly, with your own game, are you hitting your forehand well today, for example? Is your opponent getting under your skin?

Decide: In the light of your assessment of your relative performance, how should your game plan adapt? Should you start to serve-and-volley? Hit more to their backhand? Hit more slice? Play more slowly or quickly?

Act: Implement your evolved plan as best you are able.

(re)-Observe: Has the score shifted in your favour?

(re)-Orientate: ... and so on.

Written down, these are obvious, but Gilbert's success in regularly overcoming the odds show that in real life they are very effective, if difficult to do well.

The OODA loop is a powerful visualisation of how change works in practice – cycles of observation, orientation, decision and action driven by the consequential outcomes of the previous loop and the responses of your various stakeholders, competitors, colleagues and team members.

Once upon a time: the story of change

The hero's journey is a storytelling archetype that may pre-date Homer. In it our antagonist, often an ordinary, everyday soul, is called to adventure by a challenge that interrupts their life. At first they may be reluctant, then finding inspiration or unavoidable threat, they cross a threshold, in some examples such as Bilbo Baggins, literally so. Beyond this point they, and we, are drawn inexorably forward. We join them on their quest as they face great trials and conflicts, transient highs and crushing lows.

Turning back is now impossible; neither we nor they know if the world they left even remains, yet the scale of their task at times seems beyond them. They sink to their knees, head in hands. We will them on, but share their despair, their struggle seeming unwinnable. Our hero's trials present temptations that threaten to lure them from the path. In Odysseus's eponymous tale, he spent a casual twenty years diverted by all manner of threats and sexually alluring distractions on his way home from Troy. Yet at each stage our antagonist learns, gaining wisdom and skills to fortify him for the challenges to come.

At length, in the great climactic struggle that we know must come, good triumphs over evil. Our hero is ultimately victorious but is, like their world, irrevocably changed.

It is also the story of leading change.

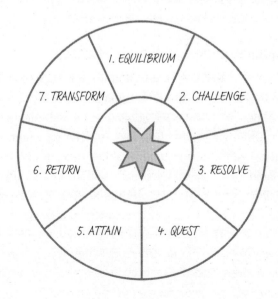

1. Equilibrium
We meet our hero in their familiar world
Bilbo Baggins in the Arcadian idyll of the Shire.

2. Challenge
Their world is disrupted by need, threat or desire
After ten years outside Troy, Odysseus wants to get home to see his wife, Penelope. (Although, at times it doesn't feel like he's trying very hard.)

3. Resolve
Our hero decides to leave their familiar surroundings and journey into an increasingly unfamiliar, unpredictable even chaotic new world.
Anna and Kristoff set out to the North Mountain to find Elsa and bring back summer. (One for the purists.)

4. Quest
As their old life drifts into distant memory they face great trials of will and endurance.
Marlin and Dory survive a jellyfish, escape a shark and ride the East Australian Current with stoner turtles.

5. Attain
At length after a climactic struggle, they achieve their goal.
Jane Eyre attains personal liberty (at least by the standards of mid-nineteenth-century Britain) by standing up to and rejecting her cruel foster mother.

6. Return
Our hero has paid a price for their victory, but at length they return to what was home.
Katniss returns from the games having survived the arena.

7. Transform
We still recognise our hero, but they are fundamentally changed by their experience.
Neo is the one who will awaken the humans trapped within the Matrix.

Examples are obvious and plentiful, from *Harry Potter* and *The Lord of the Rings* to *The Handmaid's Tale* and Dan Harmon's modern classic (yes, really), *Rick and Morty*.

Failure: an embedded feature of great success

Whole careers have been built telling tales of failure, some, it seems, achieving greater success repackaging what went wrong than they ever did in pursuit of their original goal. TED Talks and bestseller lists bulge with examples. We enjoy these stories because we learn from them, because they inspire us, but also because they fit a model with which we are very familiar.

Failures are an embedded feature of great successes. The often unspoken problem is that, when it's happening to you, right now in public, it can be deeply unpleasant, even scarring. The hole, when in it, can often feel very deep indeed. As with fictional heroes, the process will, indeed *must*, change you. You too need to resist the temptation to give up or to water down your ambitions, but also ensure you learn in order to fortify yourself for the trials to come.

I once asked Anthony Scaramucci if he had been naïve to take on the job of Donald Trump's press secretary, a role he famously held for just ten days. Scaramucci had to that point achieved an enviable level of career success. From a blue collar Long Island family, he had battled his way first into Harvard University and then into the investment bank Goldman Sachs, before establishing his own finance company, SkyBridge Capital – the embodiment of the American dream.

'Okay, so that's a funny question,' he replied. 'I was not naïve. I was naïve to the twentieth power. Any level of naïvety that you think I had, it was exponentially worse than that.'

Scaramucci had believed that he could bring order to the chaos of the Trump White House. He was quickly disabused, his public failure bringing down upon him international ridicule and opprobrium. 'When I got blown from the White House, ejected into Pennsylvania Avenue,' he told me, '[it felt like I'd been] skinned alive and then rolled in margarita salt by the late-night comedians.'

I asked him if he suffered from self-doubt, a reasonable question given this experience. 'Of course I suffer from self-doubt,' he replied. 'I'm like every other human being. But here's the thing. I'll tell you what I don't suffer from: the [un]willingness to take risk.'

Failure is hard, even if, thankfully for most of us, it is not as public as that which Scaramucci endured. However, what you must ensure is that you can experience the lows, but remain fit, healthy, happy and able to go on. As he discovered, it is not always an easy balance to maintain.

Great success is impossible without failures, often multiple and frequent. The Australian cricketer Shane Warne, arguably the greatest player of all time, understood failure as a ball-by-ball possibility, yet took each setback as an opportunity for another go. 'No matter how far they hit it, the ball always comes back,' he would laugh.

All success, including yours, will entail failures along the way. It is an unavoidable, sometimes painful, but ultimately survivable part of the process; we too will be altered at our programme's conclusion. Indeed, this must necessarily be the case, as change requires us to learn and develop in order to prevail; the new us is a consequence of all that we experience along the way. However, as John Boyd's OODA loop shows us, for our failures to move us forward, we must learn from them.

Learn to learn

When I first became a CEO, a title I had long coveted, and for which I'd been passed over several times (probably correctly, but much to my chagrin), I had, with hindsight, little idea of what I intended to do next. The title for me at that point was an end in itself, an objective gained rather than the beginning of a journey. There was, however, one thing of which I was absolutely sure. I may not have known what I was going to do, but I was 100 per cent certain what I was not. We were not going to repeat the mistakes I and others had made before me, we at least were going to make a whole load of new mistakes, ones all of our own.

John Cleese once said that success may be built upon failure, but that failure without learning remains simply that. Failure. The business I found myself in charge of was a dog, the chances of my succeeding considered by most to be slim, but I was determined that, if nothing else, we would learn – learn from what we'd got wrong in the past and be quick to learn from the inevitable missteps we would make along the way.

Sir Clive Woodward once told me that as coach he would travel anywhere, to meet anybody if he thought he could learn from them. He described himself as a sponge, eager not simply to absorb and assimilate, but to experiment and fail in pursuit of victory – victory being for him the consequence of his and his team's continual search for applicable learning and, therefore, growth.

For leaders then, it is not failure that should be feared, but rather the repetition of the same errors: the inability to learn. You're not going to be able to avoid things going wrong, but you can control the speed at which you learn.

The more I learn of leading change, the more clearly I see success being rooted in nurture rather than nature. The greatest leaders, the most successful programmes of change, are those that are able, or perhaps more importantly willing, to learn and learn fast. In the context of change, perhaps Boyd's OODA loop is simply a measure of the speed at which you learn. Woodward would assiduously analyse victory rather than agonise over defeat, a deliberate inversion of our instincts, though I'm sure defeat hurt him as much as it does the rest of us.

We enjoy hearing the hero tales of the failures of others at least partly because we gain inspiration and hope from the missteps and struggles of the successful. It's no cliché that few have achieved anything worthwhile without their share of failures along the way. A more important lesson to learn, though, is not just that it is certain to happen to each of us at different times, but to prepare ourselves and our teams for its inevitability and plan for how you're going to react. Its consequences are often not easy to overcome, quite the opposite, but at the same time, it is rarely terminal. Failure is inevitable and survivable, which is really at the heart of Cleese's and Scaramucci's message. In leading change, we must aim high, think big and learn to learn.

Change is unlearning and learning

Chapter 1 described the uncomplicated but critical process of defining and communicating your baseline. Now, finally in Chapter 8, Boyd tells us we must continually re-evaluate our position. Just as when following a map, it's not enough to know our start point and destination; we must also keep track of where we are throughout our journey. Our decisions drive action and action drives results, in outcomes both expected and unexpected, desired and undesired.

Periodic failure is an inevitable and unavoidable prerequisite of success. And failure remains just that unless we learn from it. Success must be understood, and therefore reinforced. Never, sage generals advise, re-enforce failure.

If decision drives action, then observation drives (re-)orientation.

Change can therefore be understood as a process of unlearning and learning. Unlearning old habits, processes, patterns and behaviours and learning new ones.

How we learn

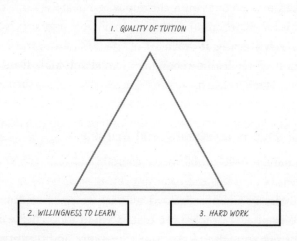

Improvement at any skill is determined by three universal factors. Imagine that you, I and a group of eight others decided today to learn a new musical instrument, one we had no previous experience of. We then reconvene a year hence and publicly compared our progress. We already know with certainty that over that time there would be significant variation in our levels of performance. This variation, however, would be driven primarily not by the chance effects of natural ability, but by three factors wholly within our control:

1. The quality of tuition

For the purpose of this thought experiment, we would each find a tutor for the duration of the year. The relative quality of this teaching would be a significant factor in our improvement. The choice of tutors has a degree of chance about it – after all, we're not experts. Nevertheless, the decision ultimately rests with us.

2. Willingness to learn

Each of us at different times would hit difficulties; we would fail, make mistakes, be unable to grasp a particular aspect of our teaching and so on. Some would be more willing or able to take direction and instruction, allowing them to more rapidly move past these blocks. This is almost wholly within our control.

3. Hard work

Some would simply try harder than others. They would turn up to all their lessons and diligently practise between them. This is wholly within our control.

At the end of the year, when we re-convened, we would discover the obvious. Some, perhaps a majority, would have made almost no improvement. They would remain complete novices. Yet some would be dramatically improved. Of course, there may be those who, through a quirk of fate, have some natural ability that pushes them on more quickly. However, as Hamilton College professor Daniel Chambliss (whose work we studied in some detail in *No Bullsh*t Leadership*) concluded, talent is simply an excuse we use to explain the performance of others.

The real difference would be determined by these three factors. Those with effective tuition, the willingness to learn and who put in the effort would perform the best. The same applies to teams, and leaders of change. It's a straight-line correlation.

In *No Bullsh*t Change* I aim to cut through the bullshit and provide direction. The other two parts are up to you. In successfully leading change, you need:

1. A clear programme **(Tuition)**
2. A willingness and openness to learn from mistakes **(Will to learn)**
3. An acceptance that successfully leading change is a marathon, not a sprint **(Hard work).**

The hero's journey is the change leader's journey. The OODA Loops are the steps you take along the way. The learning triangle shapes your baseline at the end of each loop and is how you re-orient.

NO BULLSH*T OODA

Change is not a smooth, linear process. It is a series of loops that must be completed, each requiring a fresh cycle of observation, orientation, decision and action.

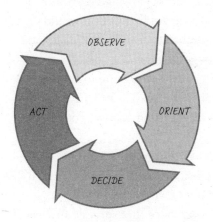

The OODA loop is a powerful visualisation of how change works in practice – cycles of observation, orientation, decision and action driven by the consequential outcomes of the previous loop and the responses of your various stakeholders, competitors, colleagues and team members. For each move you make they will make their own. To prevail, you must get inside their OODA loop.

Failure is an embedded feature of great success

Error is an unavoidable, but ultimately survivable part of the process of change. However, for our failures to move us forward, we must learn from them.

Learn to learn

The hero's journey is the change leader's journey

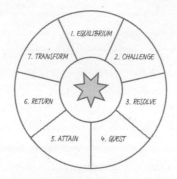

In successfully leading change, you need:

1. A clear programme **(Tuition)**

2. A willingness and openness to learn from mistakes **(Will to learn)**

3. An acceptance that successfully leading change is a marathon, not a sprint **(Hard work).**

The hero's journey is the change leader's journey. The OODA Loops are the steps you take along the way. The learning triangle shapes your baseline at the end of each loop and is how you re-orient.

CODA

The danger when leading change, is that we allow our fears to attenuate our ambition, shrinking our horizons to fit what we think we can achieve, rather than expanding them to what might be possible.

Dream no small dreams for they have no power to move the hearts of men.
Johann W. von Goethe

The secret of getting ahead is getting started.
Mark Twain

I WAS RECENTLY INVITED to take part in a panel discussion. I was late and arrived to find a rather high-brow crowd, the Chair an esteemed philosopher. Towards the end of the evening he asked each of the guests the same question: 'If you could choose with complete freedom, what would you do in life?'

I was stumped. I honestly couldn't answer. First, I tried: 'Well, I think I would spend time trying to work out the answer to that question.'

But he wasn't put off so easily. Having crossed off being a fighter pilot or an international cricketer on the basis of age (and of course ability), I eventually plumped for being either a historian or a novelist (careful to add the caveat, 'a successful novelist'). He followed up with the obvious next question, which, of course, was the real point of the exercise.

'So what's stopping you?'

The night is dark and full of terrors

The fear of failure holds many of us back. I know it does me. Yet it's mostly ill formed and shapeless: the unseen that lurks beyond the light of the campfire. These are limitations and boundaries we impose on ourselves and the ambition we have for our careers and projects. In leading change we have to accept the possibility of failure, and act anyway. As we've established, the only sure route to failure is inaction.

Like Gulliver, assailed by thousands of Lilliputians, we can find ourselves gradually, incrementally tethered by our fears and personal baggage. Often, we kid ourselves that these are the fault of others. Or bad luck. We find rational excuses to explain our negative internal narrative, making false effigies of our beliefs, blaming them for our situation. Sometimes events happen that are beyond our control, but all too often this is not the case, and of course these happen to everyone. Ever noticed how everybody else's problems always seem so much easier to solve than your own?

The danger is that our baggage and our fears attenuate our ambition. We unconsciously shrink our horizons to fit what we think we can achieve, rather than expanding them to what might be possible. In leading great, effective, enduring programmes of change, it is the latter that must drive us.

The truth is that nobody cares as much about your ambitions as you do (except perhaps your mum). This is not because people are heartless and uncaring, it's just they each have their own shit to deal with. Great mentors, great leaders, friends and colleagues can lift you up and inspire you, but ultimately it is you who must decide whether you're going to get up and do it. Doing is what takes objectives, hopes and dreams and makes them a reality. If our individual ambition is to fulfil our own potential (which, after all, is the best any of us can hope for), then we must be ever watchful that, even if we can never completely be free of the baggage in our heads, we at least limit its ability to restrain us.

It is, of course, easy to say, but difficult to do. In dark moments I imagine my foes swarming back, beavering away, tying me down. And I envisage ripping out the ropes, the tiny men flung hither and thither. Their only power is the strength I afford them and, deprived of that, they once more retreat and cower. But our watch word must be vigilance. They are nothing if not determined, and given a moments inattention the sound of tiny hammers will return.

This is not a book about career advice, and I'm certainly not about to parrot those soul-destroying Instagram memes telling you how easy it is to simply throw everything away and run off chasing your dreams. It's perfectly normal to not know the answer, or to have lots of answers, or to change your mind. Or to want be a fighter pilot. When it comes to humans, anything can be normal. And everyone wrestles with the same sort of stuff that you do.

The real question, however, is what's stopping you?

Change: an ambition with both magnitude and direction

Change can be considered the consequence of effective leadership and, in turn, all leadership concerned with effecting purposeful change. At the beginning of this book I set out the specific conditions with which it would be concerned, those when the existing order must be overturned, when revolution was needed. The modules of this programme are the steps you must take to upend that order, to set a new direction, to break free of the organisational and cultural inertia that makes change so difficult. They will guide you on how to focus on the areas that will take your programme most rapidly from ambition to reality.

These steps need not be consecutive; in fact, they are unlikely to be so. A successful change programme is typically neither linear nor quick. It is not a single giant leap, but rather a continual process. You must define direction, break free, control velocity, identify milestones and course-correct. You will take decisions that don't work, indeed it is a precondition of finding those that do. You will make bad hires, find unexpected barriers, run up against external forces (and often internal forces) that prove too difficult to shift, forcing you to think again. Markets will move, products will fail, competitors will simply outperform you from time to time. These and numberless other events are inevitable, unavoidable and, counter-intuitively, a necessary price of progress. The only way of avoiding them is to take no decisions or actions at all, to live in a permanent state of observation and orientation – we all know people who do. These are the people you want as your competitors, not on your team.

If you have got this far, you will know that the surest guarantee of failure is the failure to decide and to act. OODA loops are a simple and easy way to understand this continual interplay between action and reaction, between error and learning.

Time to begin

Here we are, all of us, standing at the beginning of a new undertaking: learning a new skill; the first day in a new role; deciding whether to change careers; with an idea for a business; just lost our job; a new project at work. We stand at the start, and the mountains tower above us.

Though we may feel alone, in fact we rarely are, we have an audience: our teams, our peers, our bosses, our preconceptions, our internal Lilliputians, watching and waiting, wondering what we will do, speculating on how we will fare. However, despite their presence, when the talking stops you must take that first step alone. The change leader's skill is finding ways to ensure that others follow – a growing and confident coalition, some of whom will in time take their turn in front.

The only sure way to avoid failure is to act; your greatest ambition, intelligent, but imperfect, progress. But that first step? That first step is always alone. Let's take it now, together.

Mail me and tell me how you get on.

Chris